THE AMERICAN DREAM
THE GREATEST NIGHTMARE

O.A. Chong

authorHOUSE®

AuthorHouse™
1663 Liberty Drive
Bloomington, IN 47403
www.authorhouse.com
Phone: 1-800-839-8640

First published by AuthorHouse 12/10/2009

ISBN: 978-1-4490-4348-3 (e)
ISBN: 978-1-4490-4347-6 (sc)

Library of Congress Control Number: 2009911938

Printed in the United States of America
Bloomington, Indiana

This book is printed on acid-free paper.

This book is dedicated to my children, in the hopes that they understand the strict disciplinary rules I imposed on them will contribute in their development as good citizens. Additionally, the educational excellence I demanded from them will facilitate their independence in this competitive world. I wish this "tough love" to be passed to their children, in order that these family values and expectations will survive the generations.

Contents

INTRODUCTION

I write this book with tears in my eyes and great sorrow in my heart. My intent is to bring to the attention and reemphasize a few values to the great majority of Americans because we have been so complacent for too many years. This state of not caring or taking any action has brought us to a point of no return, due to the decline of our country. Let this be a pocketbook, so we can read it every time we get out of line or forget where we are or what we are planning to do. We should take a step back and really evaluate our basic values, prior to making decisions that affect our lives and our whole future.

I do not claim to be a great statistician, historian, or even a scholar; nor do I have any political agenda. I do not support any political party nor have any affiliation with any specific political ideology. There will be minimal reference to names of any given individual, activist organizations, or governmental agencies/ departments in this book. If I do name any individual, I will do it with the utmost respect because they were admired by all Americans for their honesty and professionalism in their field and any mission or endeavors they set to accomplish. I am just a hard-working American that studied and analyzed the issues, seeing how this great nation has been deteriorating at a great pace with no hope of change. I will call the issues as I see them, even if this means that I will "pinch some nerves" of individuals, ethnic groups, institutions or governmental departments; sorry, but it is hard to hear and accept the truth. I am a straightforward individual with simple words, but great experiences, who has kept silent for many years. I too was part of the vast majority of Americans who care, but thought that they could not make a difference. I can no longer keep silent or I will explode. Therefore, it is time to bring to the attention of all Americans who care, that we can make a difference. I will exercise my First Amendment right given to me by the United States Constitution and voice my honest opinion. All we have to do is return to our basic principles, do something about negative points, and enhance the positive, in the name of this great Republic. I think that we owe this to our Founding Fathers and if we do not do anything about it now, they will continue to roll over in their graves.

In search of the coveted dream of success, like every other fellow American, I have worked hard, strived to receive a college education, and tried with all my might to achieve the great American Dream. However, I am scared that my children, grandchildren, and future generations will not be able to achieve this dream because it is turning into "the greatest nightmare." It is sad but true, all the aspirations of future generations no matter how hard they work and regardless of what level of education they reach, will not materialize. They will not see their dreams come true. Their educational goals will turn null regardless of the level they achieve, because the opportunities are so scarce and competition so tight that, it will be virtually impossible to reach this American Dream. To the average hard working, American this dream will be non-existent and unachievable. It is a shame but this is the true reality of what our children will be facing. Opportunities are turning into a funnel; as they grow older, it is tighter at the end because of lack of opportunities available to them.

I have served and defended this nation for most of my adult life during times of conflict and times of peace, therefore, I have earned the right to voice my opinion and express my ideas. As a citizen of this great nation, I have earned the right to complain. I refuse to complain and do nothing about the problems we are encountering in these tough times. Instead, I choose to be part of the solution and defend my rights, freedom, and those of my children one more time. It is something that I never previously regretted because this sacrifice and the experiences I gained were well worth the danger in the name of freedom and democracy. Additionally, I have had the opportunity to travel around the world, appreciate, and compare different systems of government. I came to the conclusion this is the best there is. Let us not "blow to pieces" what we have. Instead, let us fight to preserve the freedom and opportunities that we have and make the necessary changes. I have been the envy of many around the world, because I have proudly said that I was an American. Many wished or wanted to immigrate to this land to experience this freedom and opportunities that they never had the chance to enjoy.

It is a shame what we Americans have allowed in the last three decades. Due to financial greed and/or thirst for power, a few elected officials in Washington make things so difficult for the majority of hard working Americans. We have allowed these few to abuse our trust, goodwill, and level of intelligence, to ruin this great nation to the point that we are now close to a third-world country, financially and politically. We are losing out trust in the so-called "leaders" of this country, leading corporations and financial institutions. I have come to the realization that the only way this will stop is if we individually, take care of ourselves, return to basic principles, and take charge of our lives in order to make a difference. We have to fight for what belongs to us and is the legacy of our children.

After thinking things over, I have come to the realization that there are some basic issues that affect the average hard-working family in America and we should adhere to these facts if we want to be successful. I will try to list and discuss what I consider the seven most important issues, in detail as I see appropriate, because they affect all of us in the pursuit of our coveted American Dream and are the reason for our nightmare. I will repeat some basic points in each section as they intertwine during all facets of our lives. If we analyze these facts, take control of our lives, and try to improve our behavior, we can correct and learn from our mistakes, thus our standard of living will improve, and we will take charge of this country that we love so dearly. We should not depend on our government and expect our government elected officials to take care of us or assume our duties and responsibilities.

Do not allow these few to always keep us under without having the opportunity to succeed and ruin the lives of our children and future generations. We deserve better and we should demand our rights and what we deserve, have earned and worked so hard for so many years. We only have one choice and that is to make the necessary changes to our lives or suffer the consequences and allow the few to take us under with no hope of return. We have to be vigilant. Analyze issues dealt in Washington and demand from our elected officials, our right to voice our disapproval of issues that affect our lives in a negative way. Our representation in Washington should be transparent and at the approval of the people or we should replace the elected official with someone that will hear what we have to say. Enough is enough, we should be vigilant, overloading the circuits with phone calls, and e-mails, until these circuits in Washington D.C. explode whenever our elected officials do not represent us fairly. We should let them know our outrage and disagreement immediately as they try to pass legislation, loaded with pork or pet projects that we do not agree with.

MORALITY

A well-informed, properly behaved, and responsible individual makes a model or perfect citizen. Proper behavior and responsibility starts with basic training by parents in the home. People have the misconception of what morality is and usually confuse it with religious principles. Although they are closely intertwined, an individual without religious principles can have excellent moral behavior. According to Webster's dictionary, the definition of morality encompasses principles of right and wrong in behavior or ethical judgment in behavior. Religion is specific fundamental set of beliefs and practices specially agreed upon by a number of persons or sects. Sorry, but based on these two definitions, there is a lot to be desired and expected of the behavior of children, teens and adults alike at the present time in the continental United States.

I make this distinction in the definition of morality and religion because I am a firm believer in that old cliché that says that you do not discuss religion or politics because there are always disagreements and every person is always right. I am not a preacher or evangelist and it is not my intention to convert anyone. My only interest is the behavior of people in this country and how it affects one another. You can be a Christian, Jew, Muslim, Buddhist, Hindu, Atheist, or whatever you want to believe in and it is none of my concern. I just recommend you have something to believe in because it will bring happiness to your life. The United States Constitution grants you the right of freedom of speech and choice, and you should exercise this right because no one can take this right away from you. Furthermore, I want to make something perfectly clear when it comes to children and the right to bear them (which I will discuss in this section); it is also your right. I will, however, make some observations. I will not dictate my religious beliefs on anyone. Nor will I tell you the perfect way to raise your children. Neither I, nor anyone else, have this right to criticize or dictate any principles to you in the bearing of children because it is against the United Sates Constitution and we should respect the law of the land. [I make this point clear because my beliefs concern my life, not yours; the United States Supreme Court has settled this. Just remember that we all have rights and they should be respected.]

Additionally, it is not my intention to insult or criticize certain portion of the population with my conclusions of child bearing. It is a fact of life, and scientifically proven, that you need two people of opposite genders to create a life. Regardless of the procedures or methods available through scientific discoveries, it takes a part of both genders to be successful in the creating of life. This has nothing to do with the way you elect to raise this child or the composition of the family. Since the creation of this world and in every living species, this is the only possible way to reproduce or create life. I do not intend to criticize anyone's sexuality, because I respect the way people elect how, where and with whom they elect to live their lives, but as I respect your rights, I demand the same respect of my rights. I do not try to change anybody's life style but please do not try to change mine or force me to accept yours. If we live in different worlds, just live your life, be civil, and allow me to live in mine.

Nobody can dictate to you how you elect to train or raise your children; this is your right because they are your children and whatever you do with them is your business as long as you obey the laws of the land and respect others rights. I just want you to understand that sometimes we are prisoners of the rules set by our children based on the pressure of society or peers and friends that are not necessarily the best way. This is of the utmost importance in the civilized world that we try to live in. If your children's behavior affects my life, then I have the right to say or do something and take proper corrective measurement through the appropriate laws of the land. It is a proven fact that the early years of any child's life are of the utmost importance in the formation and development of their lives. We should instill certain principles, such as integrity, honesty, responsibility, and respect. We should also teach them that every individual citizen has rights and responsibilities and they should respect those rights of others. If we avoid or are negligent in providing a solid basis for the formation of our children's lives, we can consider ourselves failures as parents.

We should start with the responsibilities that we acquired when we make the decision of having children. We should have the understanding that this is a lifetime commitment of a man and a woman. Nobody else should be responsible for our children. These responsibilities also apply when we decide to adopt a child, regardless of the composition   of the family unit. We have the tendency to ignore these basic principles and blame others for our children's misbehavior. These are not toys or merchandise that we can return after having them for some time and deciding they are not what we wanted; on the contrary, they are here to stay. Let it be clear that training and proper behavior starts with the parents at home. The term "parents" does not outline detailed responsibilities for a mother or a father. It is simply a term used for dual interchangeable duties for both. You can simply be a "Mr. Mom" or a "soccer dad" and vice versa without taking your manhood away from you. It takes a lot of training, patience, commitment, and dedication to be successful in these endeavors. A babysitter or nanny is not the one responsible for the education and training of our children, because they do their best and then go home. They assist in taking care of our children on a part-time basis. Honestly, some do not really care what happens with our children after their shift is over and they go home. I am not, nor do not claim to be, a resident psychologist.

However, the years to provide our children with strong, basic, and proper behavior are between the ages of one and four. These are the years when they emulate the parents' behavior and verbal conduct. During the "formulative" years, pre-schools with twenty or more children are not the place to provide proper basic behavior principles to our children, because you lack the one-on-one contact. Yes, our children need the socialization and interaction with other children, but social interaction will not correct your child's improper behavior. On the contrary, children have the tendency to pick up bad habits from those around them. Additionally offspring, even in the animal world, emulate the behavior of the parents and siblings alike. This daily contact and interacting is lacking in today's society and we cannot blame anyone but ourselves.

It is understandable that in order to "survive" in this world today, both parents must be employed. The dual income is needed because through visual advertisement, and written and personal experiences, we have been trained to want and have the best things in life and that is what we strive to have. To some people, family is placed on the "back burner" and material things come first, which is perfectly all right, because not everyone was meant to be a parent. In this society, we have the greatest uncles, aunts, and godparents who are "part-time" parents in disguise. We must never forget that children equal responsibility and commitment. This means to learn how to do without or with lesser things in life. Are we ready to have children? Are we ready for this responsibility? Are we ready for this lifetime commitment? Are we ready for this challenge in life? If we are not, we should not bring children into this world. We should wait until we are emotionally and financially ready for this commitment. You should not allow them to acquire their morality and behavior from the TV, internet, babysitters, and/or their friends.

After this point has been settled, my interest in the children, teens, and adults is only because we live in an interactive society where our behavior affects one another. Proper behavior, sound judgment, respect, and responsibility go hand in hand and affect future success or failure in our lives. These values are a mirror for good citizenship and sometimes is lacking in our population. The

First Amendment of the United States Constitution grants us a few rights and one is speech. We all have this right and can express this right however we choose to but like the old cliché says, where my rights start everyone else's end. It should be respected and you can bet your last penny that I will demand it from others. This clearly means that your words and behavior affect me and I have the right to say something about it or put a stop to the behavior that affects or bothers me. We usually forget this and it seems that in the vocabulary of children, teens and adults, the words please, thanks, excuse me, good morning/good night and sorry have been deleted. Respect for your elders is non-existent. I wonder if it is due to the fast pace of life that we have, or the garbage we have on the internet and television or what we learn from our peers. I refuse to accept that these are the values that have been passed down to us. I also refuse to accept the fact that we do not have values or care about those of our children. Maybe it is because we have the tendency to allow our children too much without parental control, or perhaps we want to give our children more than what we had. Regardless of the reason, I am convinced that deep inside, we care, but we have not realized that it has gotten out of control.

It is completely unacceptable that children at the age of nine through twelve have more electronic equipment in their rooms than those of the working parents. It is sad that they demand this and we give in and continue to buy everything they ask for. What is wrong with introducing our children to reading as a form of entertainment? What about instructional hobbies? I find it impossible to believe that these aged children have more DVDs than books in their room. Furthermore, they are allowed to watch movies or play games in their X-Boxes that are beyond their age level. What are children who do not know how to express themselves in proper grammar doing with cell phones? How can they send thousands of text messages? What happened to "tough love"? We should be allowing our children to act their age and not push them to act as adults beforehand or allow them to fall prey to what they are exposed to; a ten-year old girl should not be dressing like a woman of twenty. We are allowing our children to dictate and set the rules in our homes. It seems that in the name of "stress" we are giving in to the rules that our children set for us. We are looking for every possible excuse to avoid the responsibility of disciplining them. Are we victims of physicians, whose solution to problematic children is to misdiagnose and keep them in a doped docile state of mind? Who is responsible for the welfare of our children, governmental agencies, or parents?

I understand that science and medicine have come a long way, but in the last three decades, the medical profession has "discovered" a myriad of behavioral problems with our children that I am surprised is not an epidemic. They start prescribing medications before the children learn how to talk. This practice continues until adulthood and all it does is create a society of prescription drug addicts. We have the tendency to solve everything with a little blue, pink, or yellow pill that has side effects, complicating our health for the rest of our lives. We have found the easiest excuse to avoid the responsibility of our children. One of the most common is Attention Deficit Disorder in which they make our children addicted to chemicals/medications from an early age. This has become one of the biggest financial gains to the medical profession, but has given us an excuse to ignore the love and attention that is needed in the home. We should try this home remedy: begin giving love and care prior to starting our children's addiction to three pills a day, only fixing the home. We should do like our parents and grandparents did for us, with one to two hours a day of love and care was the best cure all the way. We should take charge of our children's behavior and if need be, provide tough love and discipline which they will appreciate in the future.

Let it be clear that I am completely against abusing our children with belts, hands or any object. I do believe that parents are the ones who set the rules in the home. Parenting includes strict disciplinary rules, accompanied with punishment. This punishment does not mean abuse in any form. We should always stick to the punishment that is the best type of deterrent against misconduct. Taking away privileges and setting behavioral rules in the home insures that our children show excellent conduct in school and outside the home. This does not mean to send them to their rooms with all the possible electronic equipment for their entertainment as punishment. All this creates is loss of respect for the parents and for any type of punishment. Taking away their cell phones, iPods, video games, television, car keys, and going out to hang out in the shopping malls are good punishments with no abuse. If the punishment is applied and kept, our children are taught who sets the rules in the house and that these rules must be respected. Sometimes our children try us and do whatever they can think of, in order to make us lift the punishment and give in to the way they want us to be or act. We have the tendency to under estimate the level of intelligence of our children and give in to their ways. Once we do this, we lose the disciplinarian respect forever.

In order to understand the behavior of our children, I spent hours researching and observing the behavior of children at a local shopping mall and annotating the conduct of children of different ages. I set to observe males and females of the same age groups, in different occasions. To my surprise, I do not know if the parents were worse than their children were or if lack of resistance was easier for the parent. I had the opportunity to see little girls at the make-up department at a local store buying more make-up than their own mothers do. To my amazement, the mothers approved of their purchases and paid for every item that these children wanted. In my opinion, any female twelve and under is a little girl. Maybe I am from a different world but I think it is inappropriate for little girls in this age bracket to be wearing make-up, period. Continuing with my observations, they directed themselves to the clothing department to purchase the "back to school" clothing for their little girls. Again, they allowed their daughters to pick and buy every piece of clothing that they wanted. Out of respect for our youth, and having children and grandchildren of my own, I will not be crude and describe their appearance or what they looked like. Honestly, I am not a prude, but with the make-up and clothing that they purchased, their look was not a girl of that age. It was amazing that mothers allow this to happen in this great nation. I imagine that when they dress themselves with these items of clothing and wearing all that make-up they appeared to be eleven going on twenty-one. What kind of respect can another young man or a predator have for these young girls? How can we protect our children once they leave our homes? What is more amazing is the schools allow these children to attend with that attire and such masks on their faces. During my school years, in ancient times, there was a strict dress code posted prior to the start of the school year.

I like to be fair and balanced so, consequently boys are no different, but are just as bad. What I noticed is that boys have the tendency to wear clothing that is three sizes bigger than what they need. Good thing that our State has strict attire rules and does not allow boys to show their underwear outside the pants. I guess this is the "cool" look because this is what boys like today. I wonder if those boys realize that where this "fashion" comes from is prison and the true meaning of it, but if all parents rebel and don't buy this trash, fashion designers must change what they market to our kids or be in the soup line. I have tried to move along with times but some of these fashions are completely ridiculous. I do not accept that all these fashion designs are associated with ethnic groups either, because all children dress alike to fit in with their peers. It is amazing, but all around the world the great majority of the countries, children are required to wear standard uniforms to attend school. Public and private schools wear uniforms to avoid the added expenses of clothing for their children and to make it a standard dress code. This applies to all levels of schooling years of the children until graduation from high school. This also avoids the competition of different financial classes and children can concentrate on what they are going to school for, that is to study. Only in the United States of America, do activist groups claim that this is infringing on the civil rights of children. Additionally parents, under the demands of their children, do not accept this practice. Apparently, children dictate the rules and regulations of adults and schools alike. It seems that our children put more emphasis on their clothing than their studies and their priority is in dressing instead of learning. They cannot put a complete sentence together but they can claim violation of their civil rights and activist attorney groups are ready to "support these causes."

To continue my research and find out first hand what is going on, I have bought a membership for movies and music in order to have an idea of what we allow our children to watch and listen today. The violence that the movies and video games expose our children to today is far beyond my level of comprehension and I am sure that of our children. It seems that we fall into the trap of allowing our children to convince us that everything is fun and games with these video products. We are shocked when we see the news of violence that occurs in our schools and episodes of violent behavior in school transportation. These violent episodes in all levels of our school system do not occur by chance. We should stop and think that maybe these are the result of the exposure our children and young adults from Hollywood and some of the music industry. Are they prepared to separate fiction from reality? To the people who are gaining financially by the sales of this "trash," they don't care if they are able to separate these two concepts of fiction and reality because it is not their responsibility. The bigger question is why as parents-are we allowing this type of influences and behavior? As parents, we should put a stop to these practices, set the rules for our children, and allow these influences to go broke. I am sure that they will change their strategies and will produce something more constructive for our children, if we stop buying their trash. This also applies to some of the trash they call music today. Ninety percent of the words are vulgar words. They incite violence, female abuse, and disrespect for males and females alike. Additionally, the suggestions of professions for our children are not necessarily honorable ones or one that you would want to engage in. I have not heard any lyrics from these songs that make sense. The music does not qualify as a product of the Julliard School of Music. I refuse to accept the fact that all this trash is ethnic or cultural because if so, how sorrowful the future expectation we have from our young men and women. What happened to the times when we could sit and listen to a song, where the lyrics could be understood, and the melody was music to our ears? The music was multi-cultural and was composed and performed by all ethnic groups. I guess this is too much wishing and is what our children call old fashioned.

The invention of cell phones was fantastic because it allowed children to be in communication with their parents at all times. Cell phones were not invented for children to spend most of their school hours and time at home talking and sending messages to their friends. My understanding is that they were mostly recommended for emergencies and short phone calls to let parents know where their children were at all times or if they were coming home late for any given excusable reason. Nowadays children defy school rules by using their phones in the classroom for other reasons than were intended. It has been found that cell phones with cameras are used for cheating on exams and passing notes that you would not do in church. It is alarming that children today have reached the point of sending nude and risqué pictures to each other and even placing them on the internet. What is more alarming about this situation is that the age of these children, especially females, is under fifteen and an epidemic. This practice and the lack of knowledge as to the consequences of their actions have resulted in suicide attempts, suspensions from schools and problems with the law. This is linked to the lack of supervision and control by parents, or because they simply don't care. I thought that the bodies of males and females alike were like sacred temples, it is not for the whole country to see, or to share it with the whole community or the world if it is placed on the internet. We should have respect for ourselves and that includes our bodies, if we expect others to have respect for us.

Another problem is that we have become prisoners of some governmental agencies that want to dictate what, how, where and when we can discipline our children. I repeat I am completely against abusing our children in any form, way, or fashion. Children have rights and these rights should be respected at all times. I am a firm believer that our children today need tough love because every parent wants the best for their children. When a child threatens you with the fact that he or she is going to call 911 or a children's advocate agency to report you for something, because you do not allow them to do whatever they desire, there is a problem. Most of the time, the "counselors and investigators" are not qualified to perform their duties or they are overworked and do not have the time to complete efficiently a full and thorough investigation of all facts. To make the situation worst, some of them do not have children or don't have the slightest experience in the way to raise a child. It is easier to make a fast and incomplete report, find a foster home for the child, and initiate the road to destruction of any given child. Maybe that is the reason why there are so many runaways or parents that are afraid to discipline their children and allow them to do whatever they want. The result is having children that will continue down the path of misbehavior and end up in prison or with social problems.

The most painful situation for a family unit is finding out that their child is pregnant. The worst problem and most suffering brought to a parent is the sexual behavior of their children. This is the time in which parents try to find a reason why or where they failed as parents. We have an obligation to talk to our children, especially in their teen years, about sexuality. It is better for parents to take this task, instead of the schools or learning these important facts from their peers. This is not only for girls, but also applies for boys at this dangerous age. Depending with the level of communication, this should be done at a family table or individually, whichever way parents feel more comfortable. It is a shame that nowadays we have "babies making babies" without knowing the long-term damage that they do to their lives and that of their child. They initiate a domino effect of problems for their families, themselves, their child, and society. Most are likely to drop out of school and then become dependent on taxpayers to pay for the raising of their child; or become a burden to society and their family because without education they are not competitive in the jobs market. They fall into the vicious cycle of becoming dependent on government social programs. In the past, it was usually thought of only among minorities, but today it involves all ethnic groups. A few decades ago, it was an alarming situation, but we should be glad that the statistics referencing teen pregnancy have come down and are greatly improving. This could be a result of allowing our children to grow up too fast by the way they dress, put make-up and the liberties that we allow them. Again, we allow our children to dictate the rules in the house and we loose control of our children. It is a shame, but sometimes you have parents that know more about Hollywood celebrities and professional athletes' behavior and whereabouts, than that of their own children. They know the where, when, how and who the celebrities are with; but are completely ignorant of the friends of their own children and where they "hang-out" until all hours of the night. Call me old fashioned but I always believe that the teen years is to develop and socialize with friends and not boyfriends and girlfriends. I cannot understand how parents will allow their children to have friends of the opposite sex, in the name of trust, alone in locked bedrooms when they are fully aware that at this age hormones are running a hundred miles per hour. It seems unreal that there are parents that allow their children to have parties where they serve alcoholic beverages to under age teenagers in their own homes. A common excuse used is that the parents are home as chaperones and ensure that nothing gets out of line. It seems that they forget the principle of responsibility and lifelong commitment. Not to mention the laws and they should be punished worse than their children should because adults are supposed to know better. This is nothing but an invitation for trouble. Children without situations of this kind have problems with their behavior. If we provide the tools for misbehavior, we cannot expect anything good to come out of them.

I have always wondered who invented the "golden rule" that our children should be thrown out of the house at age eighteen or immediately after completing high school. Sometimes this is the formula for destruction or failure for someone that is still in the part of their years of formation. Some are simply not ready to leave the home. I fully understand that parents wish their children to be independent and able to make their own lives, but young men and women are not all the same and are all not ready for this move. Depending on the method that children are raised, they have to face a complicated world that is not very friendly and understanding to their needs. Society has lowered the adulthood to eighteen but some young men and women, based on their behavior, don't act like adults in the eyes of a reasonable person. Young adults are easy prey for the thirst of power hungry politicians; consequently, this might be the reason why they have lowered the age for adulthood and the voting age. Unless they are problem children with no hope of rehabilitation, we should offer our support unconditionally if they are trying to get ahead in life in a responsible manner. We should allow them to stay at home until they are ready to depart financially, mentally and with a formed criterion of their plans. Even in the animal world, the members of a pack stay together until they form their own pack and can live safely and independently.

As a final thought, I will leave you with a fascinating fact that is unimaginable about the laws in the United States of America. Eleven states in the union permit female minors to engage in nude dancing [and potentially prostitution] as long it is before eleven at night. This also applies to a school night. Shouldn't they have some time to complete their homework? With what can we charge these pillars of our society and owners of these establishments? Can a teenager, at the age of sixteen, have the capacity to engage in these activities? What pressure can we place on our politicians to legislate, represent us, and change these laws? I wanted to leave you with this fact and allow you to make your decision on how our nation is in great trouble with the system; and our children, teenagers, and adults' lives are deteriorating.

You should be wondering why all negative factors that I have highlighted affect the lives of our children and have something to do with the achievement of the American Dream. I have done this with the utmost respect for all the parents in this nation that are in their best compliance in the education and proper raising of their children. Sometimes we have the tendency to go blind and not see out mistakes or accept the truth when it is brought to our attention the mistakes we make with our children. The worst thing is that truth hurts and it is hard to accept, especially when an outsider tells it to us. Let it be clear that there are positive factors in our society. We should reorganize our thoughts and start correcting the negatives because these are the ones that are affecting this nation and are making "the end of the tunnel look darker." You should visualize the concept of erecting a building, without a solid foundation, the entire structure will collapse. Think of our children as the pillars that will support the structures of the bridge to the future of this Republic. First, we must understand that our responsibility is to instill in our children good behavior and conduct in order for them to become excellent citizens. Excellent citizens make the right choices and decisions. These traits will create character, conscience and will care genuinely about what happens to this nation. Second, citizens who care will get involved, will make the right choices, and be contributing elements of our society instead of a burden. We should put a stop to rewarding bad behavior with government social programs at the expense of hard working Americans. [Contributing elements to our society live a happy life and are able to achieve the coveted American Dream.] Those who are a burden because of bad choices should suffer the consequences and stop being like a ball and chain for those who obey the laws, work hard, and do the right thing for them and their families. We should treat our children according to their age, teen or young adult. Adults should set their boundaries with their children. A parent's role in a family structure is not that of a friend, but one that sets and enforces the rules and subsequent disciplinary requirements. Parents are the foundation for all family units that demand and impose rules. It is time to take a step back, return to the basics, and incorporate the words responsibility, work, abstinence, and the most important word-NO. Once we accept and understand the true meaning of these words, and make them a part of our daily lives, we are on the right track to success as parents. We should ensure that we all understand and accept our mistakes, take responsibility for them and implement corrective actions without blaming others. Yes, our children are the future of this nation and we should ensure that they do not become a heavy load or baggage to other members of our society. The most important fact is that we should ensure that they do not become dependent of the federal government because if they do, they will be controlled forever by politicians and their social programs and will never be able to leave this vicious cycle. We should instill in our children pride and independence, something they will value for the rest of their lives. Good parenting is something they will be grateful to you for, and will past it on to future generations. A vicious cycle of good parenting for future generations is a treasure that should be aspired to and admired by all.

EDUCATION

It is time to stop complaining about the educational system in this nation, get involved, and be part of the solution. Regardless of public or private educational institutions, we should remember the formula of success, which is prepared students, plus qualified educators, and parental involvement equals positive learning. Our schools are not an eight-hour day care center for students and teachers are not our high paid babysitters. I don't think there are good schools or bad or substandard schools. All schools follow a nationwide program, which is applied to all school systems within the continental United States. What we have are poor teachers who make up sub-standards schools with lack of regulatory supervision intentionally from the federal government, because of political support from labor unions. In private schools, parents demand the best teachers because they expect the best for what they are paying for. The problem seems to be parents caring or not caring, about their children's education. The schools are not what make a student's learning ability, but the learning process depends and starts with the student followed by the teachers and completed by parents. This is a proven fact because there are groups of students that always excel no matter the location of a public or private school. Those who want to take advantage of our educational system go to school to learn regardless of the adversities. There are those that just go to school to pass time, not meet the requirements, and then complain of how the system is bad. What we have to do is to concentrate our efforts into real instructional matters and leave our personal agenda aside. Activist organizations and teacher's unions should stop pushing textbooks and instructional material of religion, politics, alternative lifestyles and any other personal issues and concentrate on what students need to be competitive around the world in this century-and those that follow.

Now, there is a shortage of qualified teachers and counselors, and as it is not the most rewarding profession, our children are suffering the consequences of these shortages. Compounding the problem, since teachers have a strong union and the 'bad' teachers cannot be terminated, we are stuck with all this dead weight and our children are learning nothing. Our elected officials do not take corrective action because of political support from teacher's unions and you know the end of this story. Teachers should be required to maintain up-to-date their skills as educators and tested every two years. Those who do not maintain their proficiency should be allowed a second chance to pass a proficiency test and after two failures, they are removed. Our children deserve the best and we should demand the best for our taxes because taxpayers fund public schools. If we do not demand the highest skill levels of our teachers, failure is guaranteed. Teachers do not have standards, students do not put the required effort, and parents lack involvement and interest in the education of their children. Yet we have the gall to blame the schools for being failures and nothing but chaos. The key to success in the educational system in this nation is the parent[s]. They should demand from their children the highest educational standards, inquire about schoolwork on a daily basis, and participate in the parent/teacher programs to be informed about their children's progress. Ask to see homework assignments. If you do not take the time to find out how your child is doing in school, the teachers care less because at the end of the day they will award a social promotion due to overcrowding of classrooms or because of statistical reports to any given school district and problem solved. The truth is that sometimes we have the tendency to reward failure to give the child a "warm fuzzy." We have allowed the government to take care of the problems afterwards through social programs because we have accepted this practice for years. This is going to sound cruel but if in your household there are no high school graduates, you do not care about your child's school progress. Someone is going to take care of all of your family through a social program. There are no real consequences to the failure of the children who do not give their best effort to take advantage of the educational opportunities. There is no specific ethnic group that falls in this category and the number is growing at a rapid pace.

Taxpayers and government officials alike have criticized the educational system in this nation for decades but no solution has been offered. Little has been done for decades, to correct the problems and I am wondering why. Do you think this is the goal of some groups on purpose? Are we voters so easy to convince with their rhetoric and lies? Is their goal to have ignorant citizens who do not know better? You make your own decision. I hate to think that what they want is an uneducated population in order to be easier to control. The reasons for the doubts is that it started with the "no children left behind" program, went to the middle and presently the children are at the end of the line and still no solution to the problem. It is unconceivable that in this great nation with scholars in the field of education, a solution to the problem has not been found. Administrations from all political parties come and go and make this their top priority, but at the end of the day, nothing happens. This is the reason why it makes me think that a less educated population, dependent on the federal government, is easier to take advantage of and to control.

Our educational programs should include four basic subjects that, if we master them, will be a key in the success of all citizens in this great nation. It will also enable us to avoid future embarrassments and failures in our lives. We must demand that our children are able to master reading, writing, analytical thinking and arithmetic or math. We should ensure that these basic subjects are taught in elementary, middle and high school. We should ensure, prior to passing to the next level, our children are proficient in all these areas. Once our children reach proficiency in these subjects, I guarantee that they will avoid failure in any endeavor. In the future, they will be able to read all documents that they sign and figure all financial obligations to which they commit themselves. I will refer to these four subjects in future chapters in order to understand and demonstrate the linkage to everything we do in life. Failure to master these skills will result in negative consequences because everything we do in life is based on these four subjects. We should compliment these subjects by incorporating history, geography, the arts [and music], social studies and physical education for the health and welfare of our children. All physically fit children are alert, grasp concepts better, and are an overall better student. Teachers and parents often complain that long session days are too much for their children but an eight-hour day of dedicated work in school is not too much to ask from our children. The average American is required to work eight hours a day, consequently why not demand it from our children, when it is correlated that their job is to study. Additionally, with good counseling we must also consider the ultimate educational goal of the student to add science, chemistry, enhanced mathematical skills and continued physical activities to the curriculum. These subjects should be considered at high school when the student determines what his or her final educational goals are.

We must accept the fact that not all students are college material. Parents should stop the tendency to guide their children towards the parents' personal goals. Early testing will determine who has the determination, dedication, and intellectual skills to pursue a college education. Those that have vocational skills should receive or be enrolled in a vocational program in order to avoid frustration and failure. Students who are frustrated have problems with learning and no interest in school, will fail to advance academically, drop out of school, and be a burden to society. Not everyone was born to be a physician, lawyer, or a scientist and we must accept these limitations. There are good individuals that master skills that require working with their hands i.e., mechanics, electricians, carpenters and plumbers. These respectable professions earn a good, honest, and decent living and are always needed. The biggest mistake that parents commit is not to accept the limitation of a child, consider them a failure, and convey this thought to their children. There is a tendency among the American people in which we try to gear our children toward accomplishing what we were not able to accomplish ourselves when we were young and had the opportunity. There should be no embarrassment if our children elect to be a blue-collar worker or because we cannot show them as a prize trophy among family and friends. It is better to work in a field where we are happy and successful, rather than being a professional where we are frustrated and hate to go to work on a daily basis. Money is not everything in life; it helps some, but it does not buy happiness. This frustration will create a high level of anxiety and stress that in turn, will elevate your blood pressure, could lead to drinking and in the end; you become a failure with medical problems. A great number of homeless individuals are white-collar professionals that were frustrated with their choice or line of work; that is a fact.

Regardless of what program of study the student elects, the "basic four" should always be taught plus the complimentary four. No matter what we do in life we, must specifically, know how to read at an acceptable level. We must also be able to understand what we are reading, not just reciting words. We also need be able to write and express our thoughts in a coherent manner, to include, being able to spell and write a complete sentence. These two go hand in hand because it facilitates oral expression in which others can understand what we are trying to say with a complete thought. You would be surprised to learn that, if it were not because of "computers," some college students and professionals would not be able to express themselves or graduate from college. College students can classify the "computer spell check" program as one of the wonders of the world. Amazingly, some professionals in "certain" fields would not be able to survive without this program. We should know basic arithmetic and, if possible, some mathematics without the use of an electronic calculator. Students are required to pass a Standard Achievement Test to enter college and are allowed to take the test with the help of a calculator and word spell electronic machine. We know what these machines can do but, what about our students.

The Standard Achievement Test is to find out what a student knows or has learned through his or her basic education. I am sorry to say this but this test is a farce. The reason I make this statement is that our society encourages our population not to be honest. There always is going to be someone who challenges the rules, very careful not to break them, in order to make money. For every test that challenges your mental capacity, there is a sample test to prepare you to pass it. After you practice a myriad of sample questions, by the rule of average, you will pass the real test. I do admire those students that dedicate hours, days, and years to practice these tests in order to pass the real thing. We should be able to analyze all the material that is presented to us even though we are not rocket scientists. You do not need a postgraduate analytical mind to read and digest basic concepts in life. This means to read, understand what is read and formulate an intelligent conclusion of what we read in order to make a decision. If you are a white or blue-collar worker, you need the basic four in order to be successful in life.

One of the complimentary four subjects needed in the education of our children is history because we should always be versed in the roots that formed our nation. In history, we can incorporate the study of civics because it is also part of our history. This is of the utmost importance because young men and women should be fluent in the area of civics, as it will prepare them to vote and elect the "leaders" of this nation in the future. This will give the knowledge, preparation and all the understanding of our form and branches of government. We should understand the principles and intentions that our founding fathers had when they finalized and instituted the Bill of Rights and the US Constitution. This will provide instruction to us in how to respect others rights and demand that our rights be respected. People have the tendency to forget that freedom and rights are a two way street and should be reciprocal. Something those two very important principles incurred were duties and responsibilities that are a part of being a citizen of this nation. We should get out of the mode that we just exist in our own little world, we are part of this nation, and we should get involved in the process for the benefits of all. Additionally, we must make our children aware of discrimination, the Civil Rights movement, all the wars and conflicts that our nation have been involved, and other events that have affected our nation. If we have knowledge of all these events, we appreciate our rights and freedom and will give respect to others and demand the same respect back. We should create awareness to ensure that the same events, wars and periods of atrocities, do not occur again in our nation. If we are well rounded with all this knowledge, then we should render our utmost support to government officials. We should actively participate in prevention, in order so these episodes do not happen again in our nation and around the world. We should ensure our children understand that as a super power, we serve as a model for freedom, civil rights and liberties and democracy around the world. We should also make them aware of the reason why we have become involved in other humanitarian missions around the world.

Geography is as important as history because some students, adults alike, cannot even find their location on a map of all fifty states. Shameful, but true, that this is an indisputable fact today. Some people are convinced that America is a country and not a continent. They do not even know that the continent is divided into three Americas. If you talk or ask a question about Europe, Asia, South West Asia, Africa, etc., they are perplexed. What is a shame is that the American people have the intelligence to learn, but have been led to believe that the only thing important in the world is America. All this lack of knowledge contributes to being less competitive with other nations in the world. We have been trained not to see past our noses and cannot comprehend that it is great to be able to understand that there are other people, cultures, and languages around the world besides English, Rock and Rap music. Some people's knowledge is limited to Canada, Mexico, and some Caribbean Islands because that is where they vacation, what they watch on television and that is where it stops. What is hilarious is that most of the ethnic groups in the United States of America have the tendency to demonstrate their ethnical "pride" through the use a hyphenated name before American to identify themselves or their roots. However, they do not know where that country or continent is on a map. If they would be able to identify the location on a world map their pride, would increase, as they will comprehend the suffering that their ancestors went through to come to this nation. Personally, I do not approve of this practice because we are all Americans period and should be proud of it. The Constitution does not speak of a hyphen American but only one American, with no exception. When you start using a hyphenated name before American, it gives the impression that you are not proud of this nation and something is lacking. Although some people have the need to be different, if they have the knowledge, this will also help students understand which nations are friendly and which hate our standards and system of living or what we stand for. Additionally, it will help our children understand the value and reason we get involved in preserving freedom and democracy around the world.

Arts and music have been proven to enhance the motor skills of students. Enhanced motor skills will assist in the ability to pursue studies the in scientific worlds, which are based on advanced mathematical equations. These mathematical skills are important for those who seek a career in the medical field, engineering, biology, chemistry, or science. These fields are in constant need by this nation. These two subjects also open cultural horizons and give students an opportunity to learn other cultures and languages, which are an advantage in the global markets. A person who is multi-lingual has the advantage in the competitive world job market. A student exposed to the arts and Music will be a well-rounded, cultural individual. Individuals that are able to read music also show that they are capable and develop a special facility to comprehend complex mathematical theories and subjects. These two fields provide the opportunity to enhance their cultural horizons and participate in student exchange programs, which will give them an invaluable myriad of experiences. These will open the doors to the world and will give them an incentive to participate in unique world programs such as the Peace Corp and serve the nation as an ambassador of the United States of America to the world. This service will help them acquire values, responsibility and help them appreciate the freedom and opportunities that this nation has to offer. This will diminish the dependency from the federal government and will teach them how to earn, work, and value their independence.

All schools should have a mandatory amount of time dedicated for physical education. At the rate that our students are suffering from obesity and premature medical complications at a young age, they should have supervised physical activities at all grades during their entire educational process. Physical activity, plus preventive medicine equals brighter and more alert minds. Healthy students have a lower amount of absenteeism and will participate and perform better in the classroom environment. This is not meant to be a pass to prepare students for professional sports, as a decline in dedication to other curriculum requirements, results in failures and social promotions. Although it is a common belief that organized sports, teach our young men and women discipline and cohesiveness. If they are not successful or achieve the professional level, where is the reward, when they can barely convey their thoughts, communicate in a complete sentence, or convey their thoughts to a level that they can be understood? Regardless of the argument that most will offer, it is common that knowledgeable jocks and social promotions go hand in hand. Most jock's written and oral skills leave a lot to be desired and the positions in television for sports announcers are far and few. These programs should be geared only for the health and welfare of students, to ensure that later will not shoot the cost of medical insurance sky high.

I firmly believe that we should prepare ourselves to provide the educational needs of our children. That comes with the responsibility and preparation of having children. The federal government is not responsible for our children and that should be perfectly clear. I do not agree that a student pursuing attendance to an institution of higher learning should incur a debt of thousands of dollars prior to entering in the work force. This does not mean that we should not support our children that want to pursue these goals. We should fully understand that times change and nowadays a high school diploma is not enough to be successful in the competitive job market. These are not the times of our grandparents and parents when a high school diploma was a commendable achievement. At the rate we are going, a college degree often is not enough in certain professional fields because the world has become very competitive. In certain fields, it is mandatory to attend graduate school, to be competitive. For those parents that have not put in place a long range plan for their children, student loans are the only avenue available for their children. I am sorry, but the student loan program is an excuse for the parents' lack of planning for their children's education, regardless of your income. We should start saving for our children's education upon making the decision of bringing them to the world. It is completely unfair to put our children through the burden of incurring a debt of such magnitude before they are able to earn a living. Today a student will have to repay a student loan for ten or fifteen years if they attend a name university under this program. They will not incur this debt if they attend a community college and transfer to a state university, which might not include the top name universities in the nation. Regardless of what politicians will preach, promise, or lie about providing a lower interest rate to alleviate the burden on students, this is an immense debt to place on our children. With or without a low or decent rate of interest, they have to pay it back. The paying back of the loan is contingent upon if the student is lucky to find a job upon graduation, which, depends on the field he or she chooses to study. At the rate our economy is going, a student is lucky if he or she can even get a student loan approved. The biggest joke now is that politicians promise young men and women that everyone will have the opportunity to attend college, as if it was free. What is sad is they target the young for their vote and many students are under the belief that the federal government is going to provide a free education. If you are attending school today, to make it simple just multiply the cost of your education by the number of students in your class. If you have mathematical skills, you estimate the number of students in your school and then multiply that number. Then you use your imagination and "guesstimate" the number of universities and colleges, to include community colleges, in the nation. When you come with a number, you will understand. The federal government is not going to provide you with a free education and the promises of politicians go with the wind. If they are just promising a low interest student loan, at the rate the interest rate of banks with this economy, they are not doing you any favors. Sorry, you are very intelligent because in order to attend college you had to score high in your Standard Achievement Test, but they are taking you for a fool or for your vote with empty promises. This applies to politicians of both parties no matter what your political science professor says or what political ideology you have. I just want to make it clear that I am not insinuating who you should vote for because it is none of my concern. I personally do not believe in politicians, because all politicians of both parties are the same and they only care about themselves, their party agenda, and special interest lobbyist. They don't care about you, me, or the American people as a whole, so you continue to vote whichever way you want to.

I will touch another big nerve of some people because no matter what our children achieve scholastically, the only alternatives they have are to pay out of their own pockets or student loans. Scholarships are very few and only given to those "chosen ones" under Affirmative Action or sports jocks which is a school publicity gimmick. The subject of Affirmative Action and our government will be discussed later. Something that I am completely against, because we are all Americans and equal opportunity should apply the same to everyone. Scholarships should be awarded on scholastic merits and not on quotas, origin, creed, religion, or ethnical groups. Although there is no such thing as reverse discrimination, the same principle of discrimination applies when you start giving preference to one group of people or the other. When you start applying these special standards to "level the playing field," you create a state of mediocrity in the educational system. This is a creation of our politicians and has been accepted by a corrupted society for years, for fear of being labeled as a racist or accused or racism, people elect to keep quiet. Sometimes high achievers cannot even apply, attend or be accepted to the universities of their choice because these institutions go from A to Z, accepting the "elite" and the "quotas" so they can qualify for federal assistance. Unless you happen to be a "jock," to enhance the school or university's sports team, the elite or be a member of the right population, your chances of being accepted to the school of your choice is zero to none. The average American's doors are limited or completely closed when it comes to applying for any named university because the funds or opportunities are not the same across the board. The only other alternative or assistances our children have are Pell Grants and Tuition Assistance. In order to qualify, you have to be part of the lowest financial spectrum. If you work hard and make a decent living, your children will not qualify for Pell Grants or Tuition Assistance because of the parent's income, regardless of their scholastic achievements. Another joke is that even organizations that offer scholarships or any type of assistance will apply the same standards, rules, and requirements to award this assistance to students or how they manage these programs. It is becoming clear that everything in the United States of America is based on quotas and that the merits or level of qualifications or intelligence is non-existent. This is what we call the great American Dream and the land of equal opportunity, and this we owe to our elected officials. Sometimes our children work hard scholastically, but if their parents do not plan, they will face disappointments. Maybe the idea is to stay dumb, be a bum, and leech off the federal government in order for politicians in Washington to control our lives.

Children who have the scholastic abilities should not be discouraged if they do not accepted to named universities or get the needed financial assistance. They should pursue their goals through what they can afford, even if that means to start through state community colleges. At the rate the price of higher education is going, sometimes this route is better for some students because it is based on their own efforts. Additionally, classes are smaller and they have a better chance to receive a personalized instruction and better grasp concepts. Transferring to a state university afterwards is perfectly acceptable and easy, if they maintain a good grade point average. The key is when you attend college, you have to be committed and responsible to study and give your utmost effort. I will encourage students to stay at home, at a local community college and then transfer to any school once they have experienced the attending an institution of higher learning. Please do your research based on what is the best school for your field of study, but please don't base your standards on the football team they have or the name of the school. Unless you want to be a politician and have to go to law school and "flash" the name of the four major schools in the nation, which I won't mention their names. A named institution does not mean that knowledge is going to be transferred to the student automatically. Regardless, where you attend school (the dedication in your learning, the study habits what you put into it) is what you get out. Remember that when air goes in, the only thing that might stay is air and air comes out. The only thing automatic is what you have to pay to attend a name university, but not what you get out of it. Regardless of where you get your education from, you have to prove your knowledge and qualifications upon graduation and at your place of employment unless you are a "quota" and you do not even have to show for the interview. Remember that only in politics, the judicial system, Wall Street, and the media must you "show off" or "flash" the name of the school you attended.

I will continue to honor my pledge of not naming any institution, but I have known and seen individuals from named universities that are "dumber than a rock" with no common sense and it seems that they went to college, but the learning did not sink into their brain. Sorry for being so blunt, the only thing that these individuals learned was to kiss butt, rub elbows with higher ups and lie, cheat or backstab everyone on their way to the "top." In contrast, people from smaller schools are brilliant, honest, team players and with great abilities in their chosen field. I will touch another nerve, there are some institutions that have a "special political agenda," with worthless professors, and all they are interested in is the assistance they receive from the federal government or special interests donations. There a great number of these institutions of higher learning around the nation and some don't care and don't hide it. I do not need to pay thousands of dollars to get my child "brain washed"; I can do that at home free. Additionally, I expect the highest standards demanded from my child while he or she is in school. Not just "pass and review" as long as I pay or have my child in school until he/she leaves in a wheel chair or ready to collect Social Security. If I want my child to experience "Sodom and Gomorra" for thousands of dollars, again I can allow that for free at home and maybe with higher standards because I can supervise that his/her behavior and will not have an illegal or drinking habit. I am not generalizing and although I am not a statistician, there is a sixty/forty percent of this happening in named universities and it is not publicized by the media because this is part of "growing up," independence and socialization. I am not a psychiatrist, but your bad behavior does not stop at Spring Break, it continues during weekdays, weekends, and holidays. I am not too impressed with the credentials that certain individuals claim to have from these special named universities because some fall into the category of "dumber than a rock." Americans have the tendency to gloat and flaunt the names of the schools they have attended for their higher education. Maybe the institutions are proud because of individuals that claim they graduated from these schools hold positions in high places. It makes you wonder how they got there and if it was because of their brain or degree of intelligence. There are a great number of smart, dedicated, and responsible students that attend school for only one purpose; that is to learn and take advantage of the opportunity given to them. They are grateful of the effort that their parents made to defray the cost of their higher education. These students attend a great number of named and small colleges or universities; that is why the name of the school is not important. What is important is what you get out of the instruction you receive.

It is important that we fully understand why education is one of the key factors that affect the achievement of our American Dream, because this is what makes our children and us competitive in the world job market and put us at a level equal to other nations around the world. A rounded educational program with qualified teachers/ professors will prepare our students to face any challenges in life. We are facing horror stories where we have unqualified teachers and professors in all levels of our educational institutions, that are receiving high salaries without performing their duties. In our higher educational system, we have professors with special political agendas, which I consider out of place because you do not have to spend your life savings on your children to get this non-academic political agenda in the name of forcing them to think. It is shameful that this nation, as powerful as it is and trying to be the example to other nations around the world, is not ranked in the top ten in the world when it comes to education. We should demand the best educational system from our local and federal government elected officials because our children are intelligent and they only need the opportunity to excel. Politicians, teachers, and professors work for the taxpayers not for teachers unions or lobbyists of special interest in Washington. The cost of education from elementary to high school is not cheap and presently is a waste of our taxpayer's monies because of unqualified teachers and lack of parental involvement. The cost of a college education is too high, some parents make a special effort to support their children to attend these institutions of higher learning, and we cannot accept mediocrity. We are supposed to have the best educational institutions in the world, but that is a fallacy because in many cases all we have is a school name with unprepared or unqualified graduates. There is a shortage of doctors, registered nurses, engineers, scientists and we are forced to recruit personnel from other countries to fill the existing vacancies in this nation because our students cannot or are not prepared to perform these duties. It is hilarious that we have the tendency to call these countries as "third world nations," but this is where we get the personnel to supply our needs. Our students have the tendency to get into the fields of business or economics and political science in order to become lawyers because they want to get into the three best "gigs in town," Wall Street, politics and the judicial system. These fields of financial greed, thirst of power and judicial system are where people can borrow, lend, and steal with no consequences. These three protect each other without penalties, because they make their own rules and laws. These individuals think that they are above the law and "we the people" do not demand any type of accountability. I do not like to generalize when it comes to a population or profession, but we have become prisoners of lawyers because they have turned into the cancer of this society. They have become a detriment to our system of government and cost of medical care, because of frivolous suits and they have corrupted the Judicial System altogether. The lack of trained personnel in other fields, especially science, has resulted in the outsourcing of many industries to countries where personnel are available and trained.

This has resulted in less opportunities of employment at all levels of pay and skills. If there are fewer jobs in this country because of lack of trained personnel, and competition for the high technical or paying jobs is almost non-existent and corporations leave the nation, we cannot blame anybody but ourselves. I am sure that you have heard the saying "easy come, easy goes" and this applies to jobs with no trained personnel. This affects the American Dream because less jobs are available and opportunities that remain in the United States are minimum wage jobs which are a detriment to our capitalistic system, system of government due to lack of tax revenues, promotes more dependency on social programs, larger government control and less freedom to our citizens. We know better and have the capabilities to make the right decisions when it comes to selecting and electing our government officials. We have to wake up and start demanding what we and our families deserve in this nation. We are reaching the point of no return and it is time to put a stop to all the abuse from our elected officials. Our tax monies are not to be utilized as their personal funds for pork or pet projects and to satisfy special interest in Washington, but in the betterment of our children's education. Additionally, we should put a stop to the practice of satisfying the demands of activist organizations instead of opportunities for all the American people.

IMMIGRATION

It is a proven fact that the American people have a "heart of gold" and are always ready to assist anyone around the world in a time of need. However, this "golden heart" has been tarnished because, although we welcome all immigrants, the illegal immigration problem has gotten completely out of hand. This is a problem that has been going on for decades and the politicians only sugarcoat it without a solid solution to the problem. I make the comparison to a "kid in the candy store" because of the availability of votes from the Hispanic community and with simple, false promises, they continue to manipulate them. How many times do we have to offer amnesty to illegal immigrants before we find a permanent cure to the illness? When are we going to protect our borders finally? What is the hidden agenda of the politicians?

I am a firm believer of legal immigration, because immigrants who came to this land for freedom and opportunities founded this country. Although many of the readers might think that I have radical ideas, I will make a disclosure and let you know that I am a product of legal immigration. I liked what I saw when I came to this country as a student and made the decision to return to this country legally, that is the right way. I did not overstay my student visa, but returned to my homeland, processed the necessary documentation and waited my turn to return legally to the United States. I did not break any immigration law nor have been a burden to this nation, on the contrary, I have contributed more to this nation that some native-born. I am proud to be an American citizen and proud of my service to this nation. I make this disclosure to show an example that if you do things the right way, you avoid having any humiliation or painful consequences later.

The immigration laws need revision and then enforced and applied to every individual with no exceptions, immediately. It will be helpful if quotas for countries are increased in accordance to what we can accept or assimilate from each country, if the immigrant will be independent and will not be a burden to the nation. You should be able to provide proof of a career or profession and if these jobs are available for that skill in the continental United States. This will alleviate some of the problem of illegals overstaying their tourist visas or coming to this nation, illegally crossing our borders. The exception to the law that states that those individuals from "special countries" can stay if they reach land should be eliminated. This applies to all from the Caribbean Islands that receive this special treatment from clauses in the immigration laws. The law is the law. It should be applied the same way to everyone, because all illegal immigrants reach American soil anyway, and stay. Those that request asylum based on political persecution is completely different. The section that states that an immigrant can pass the legal status to relatives, i.e., father, mother, and siblings should be revised because this will create a "snowball effect," instead of granting legal status to one person, it will turn into one hundred. If you are caught illegally in this country regardless of the circumstances, you should be deported, penalized and suffer the consequences. This should include "arranged" marriages where the legal citizen should serve time in jail and the illegal deported. If you establish a family knowing that you are breaking the immigration laws, you should still suffer the consequences. This is not ignorance of the law but defiance of immigration laws expecting sympathy in the application of the laws. The laws are not applied with the heart, but the way they are written, and should be respected and enforced. The argument that immigration officers are "breaking families" is not a special category or clause within the immigration laws. The excuse that you have children born in the United States does not give you the right to stay here because you intentionally broke the laws. You were aware of the consequences of your actions and that does not fall under the category of a hardship. Hardships are when circumstances happen out of your control and without direct input on your part. Bad choices have terrible and sad consequences and punishments as dictated in the law. If the law calls for deportation of the whole family, let it be. The children should be given the opportunity to return after age eighteen and elect to be American citizens and to return with no restrictions. Some illegal immigrants are in a hurry to have children born in the United States, to have the excuse that their children are Americans, to be treated with compassion. Thinking with the heart and compassion has a limit, especially when it is creating a major problem within the nation. Demonstrations and protests, activist organization pressures or religious pleas should not make a difference in the enforcement of the law. Activist groups are working for politicians and the countries where the illegal immigrants come from, because it is in each party's best interest. To a great number of individuals this might sound like a heartless position, but this is the treatment you will receive around the world if you stay illegally in any country. Thus, the same should apply in the United States of America. These rules should apply to all immigrants from all parts of the world with no exceptions. All illegal immigrants deported to their own country should be required by law to wait at least fifteen years prior to being considered for legal entrance to this nation, even if applying for tourist visa. If you break the immigration laws, it is a felony and should be enforce to the maximum extent of the law. If an American citizen commits a felony, he or she is tried and punished. This same principle should apply to illegals. What is confusing is that our Southern neighbor applies the stiffest penalties to those that break their immigration laws. It has been documented that individuals from nations further south initiate their journey to "gringo land" are persecuted, jailed, fined, required to pay bribes and even murdered or disappear at their border towns. These crimes are committed in the name of border protection, application of immigration laws and protection of the nation's sovereignty. When it comes to the laws of the United States, border protection, and sovereignty is thrown to the wayside in the name of compassion and comprehensive immigration. It seems that the activist organizations are mute to these accounts or they apply the rule of "don't do as I do but do as I say" to justify the abuse in this nation.

Now, Hispanics are the fastest growing minority population in the United States. Legal immigrants within the Hispanic community have the tendency to vote with solidarity and support the causes of fellow Latinos. Politicians know, understand and take advantage of this situation and see the Hispanic community as a political gold mine. It is sad to say but usually the level of education of Hispanics is not the highest and they see the federal government as a means to obtain their necessities. Politicians, making all kind of promises, but doing nothing about the real problem, target this voting group. They do not try to put a stop to the root of the illegal immigration problem, because they want to take advantage of this sector of the population as long as they can. How many times will politicians award amnesty to illegal immigrants? What is the magic number of illegal immigrants needed before something is done about this problem? It seems that politicians are going to "milk this cow" as long as they can, or until it gives "powdered milk." As long as they can control this population, they will "toy" with them until the next wave of illegal immigrants are in the country and start the vicious cycle again. Usually they start "finding" a solution to the problem as the new election cycle starts or the political campaign is ready to kickoff. The new theme of the solution by politicians is "comprehensive immigration" with respect and humanitarian principles. Fourteen to twenty million illegal immigrants is an enormous number to assimilate into the system because it will create a "domino effect" on benefits; government approved social programs and jobs. This number was calculated many years ago, but now it has multiplied, because most illegal immigrants have a family of four. Sometimes it makes us wonder if politicians comprehend the sentiments of those that have to pay for all the expenses that illegal immigrants create to taxpayers.

Now, many states with southern borders are suffering with their budgets, because illegal immigrants are receiving social benefits at a gigantic rate. This includes social, medical, and educational requirements that the states cannot provide within their budget. I will touch another nerve with the following comment. Hispanics have the tendency to reproduce at an alarming rate, which is the reason they are the fastest growing minority in the United States. The medical and educational needs of Hispanics will break any state budget. The medical needs received at emergency rooms of most hospitals, run the deficit into the hundreds of millions of dollars. We should remember that one of their goals is to have American-born children in order to circumvent the immigration laws by having kids who are American citizens. The special educational needs such as English as a second language and special education teachers, also break a state's budget. It is now to the point where our "great politicians" want to give free college education, under the guise that they need to be trained and given the opportunity to avoid being a burden; something that American citizens cannot receive and are often not able to afford. The excuse that we have to "level the playing field" is a poor excuse, which makes me sick. This "playing field" is only for special people because they are here illegally in the first place and, why should we bend over backwards for someone who has broken the law? Does the student loan program apply to them? If it is because of lack of documentation, then they need to get on the first airplane leaving the United States and get their higher education in their homeland. Until what point are we going to allow the politicians to insult our degree of intelligence, trying to justify their agenda at our expense.

The first step that we must take to correct the illegal immigration problem is by seriously securing our borders. Many think that illegal immigrants only cross via the southern border of the United States, but illegals have gotten smarter and now fly to Canada and cross via the northern borders. It is easier to cross because of the lack of border officers. It is true that most illegal immigrants come from Central and South America because they are seeking a better life and opportunities and they cross the southern border. The amount of money they earn here in one day would take months to make in their native land. That it is why they try so many times to cross the border. If caught, they will continue to try until they are successful. A vicious cycle will never stop until our politicians are serious in securing our borders. They are persistent because their necessities can be fulfilled and the opportunities available in this country for them are innumerable. To many, they are convinced that every American has a "money tree" in their back yard, and instead of leaves, it has dollar bills. Every day there is more pressure from these countries, Hispanic politicians, and activist groups from these countries for Congress to pass a comprehensive immigration law. One of the reasons is because the largest industry that these countries have is the money illegals send back to their countries to support their families. This boosts their economies. The American dollar is the salvation to a great number of these countries, although they are not friendly towards the United States. Amazingly, the American government does not realize the dollars from illegal immigrants sent home to support and keep in power many "dictators" in Latin America. This is the reason why a great confusion comes to my mind at the opposition from politicians to secure our borders. I understand that the votes that they receive from the Hispanic community will secure their political careers in Washington, but I hate to think that there is another hidden agenda. With all the technology we have in this country, it should not be difficult to secure our borders. Additionally, if we send our military personnel overseas to secure freedom for other nations, why are we not allowed to use the military to ensure that our own people's freedoms are secure? Additionally, it is hard to understand why our military and border patrol officers are not able to utilize their firearms to protect themselves, or the lives of citizens around the border communities with all the criminal behavior of drugs and human trafficking. It is shameful that officers are prosecuted if they perform the duties that they were sworn to do. How many law enforcement personnel will have to loose their lives before we do something about this problem? Furthermore, the word and testimony of the criminals around the borders have more value in the eyes of justice. It leaves a lot to be desired of our criminal justice system in the United States, when criminals have more rights than law-abiding citizens. I ask myself the same question repeatedly, is there something else that the average citizen doesn't know about the border security or illegal immigration saga. It is hard for a person with a brain to comprehend the reason why this problem has not been solved for decades. Some might think that I am a pessimist, but with so much corruption in "high places" in our government, maybe some or a few are receiving benefits from arms dealers and drug traffickers because our government officials are not necessarily saints or angels. Again, with all the technology available in this country, it is virtually impossible and unconceivable that these problems on our borders have escalated to an uncontrollable level. I will leave that to your own judgment and conclusion because it does not sound or smell good.

The argument that illegals pay taxes is one that has me perplexed. How can you pay taxes, if you are not allowed to work in this country? If they are using stolen identities or illegal documents to work, they are committing a double crime. Being here illegally and falsifying documents. Now, our federal government is one of the major contributors to the illegal immigration crisis. They have allowed illegal immigrants to obtain a personal identification card for paying income tax and this is outrageous. They can justify their stay in this country illegally because they state that they are contributing to the nation and are entitled to federal benefits. It is a proven fact that identity fraud is one of the fastest and most devastating crimes in the continental United States today. Not only do you ruin the lives of those whose identity is stolen, but make them prisoners with a life sentence. This is a crime compared to homicide because the person losing their identity has lost his or her life. Why can we not have our governmental agencies exchange information in order to verify unscrupulous practices by criminals? Why are certain governmental agencies forced to remain silent when they become aware of an illegal immigrants' status? Why do politicians fight with all their might approving a national identity card? I fully understand that politicians do not want a national identification card, because that will decrease the opportunity of voter's fraud. Those registered, by activist organizations more than one time, from state to state and those who are not eligible to vote will stop. That will be a blow to those marginal politicians, for whom this is the only way that they can win elections. This will alleviate the problem with identity theft, fraud, and falsification of documents for illegal immigrants to obtain employment. In addition, it will prevent fraudulent Social Security applications, obtaining a driver's license and most importantly, application for social benefit program that are taking this nation to the cleaners. The authorities should also triple the penalties to those employers who refuse to verify information presented by potential employees. This is part of the sickness that this country is experiencing, because employers in their greed, or unions looking to enhance their members, will hire or allow illegal immigrants. Their penalties should be increased, because it gives the impression that they "pocket" the taxes that they deduct from the salaries of these illegal immigrants. To who is, the salary taxation credited? What are the effects on the life and benefits of the individual's stolen SSN? These employers are as guilty as the illegal immigrants that break the laws to come in this country. We know the union, who gets the dues, directly funnels those to lobbying the politicians. Could it be that these employers make large donations in support of a politician's election or reelection campaigns? If politicians claim that national identification and exchange of information between government agencies is too expensive, maybe they should stop their pet and pork programs for one year they can defray the cost of all these programs that the American people need and affect their lives. Maybe I am too bold to make a comment or statement of this nature.

The other famous activists' excuse is that illegal immigrants come to this country only to perform jobs that Americans do not apply for or want. The only job that most Americans might not want to do, is, working as farm hands. However, not all illegal immigrants are farm hands and most do not want these jobs anyway. There are no farms in front of major hardware stores or on the street corners of major cities within the United States. This is an excuse from social activists and employers that do not want to pay a decent wage for a decent day of work. They take advantage of illegal immigrants because they have few or do not realize they have no rights and will take whatever pay they can get. This is much better than what they would be able to earn in their homeland. Additionally, illegal immigrants will take any abuse because they are afraid of being deported, so these employers take advantage of this situation and abuse them. One thing is clear, most illegal immigrants are good, hard workers and they come to this country to work and find a better status for their family. The problem is that they are here illegally and that is against the law. The excuse that they only take jobs that Americans do not want is not necessarily true because if your family is hungry, you cannot pay bills and are suffering; I am sure that if you are responsible you will take any job that is available to you. If that job is in a meat packing company or any type of factory work, you will take this work because any job is better than no job. I am also sure that you will take two jobs, if necessary to take care of your family. The only reason you will not take this course of action, is if you "leech" from the federal government and being an able body will abuse social programs and the system. This might apply to a portion of the population, but not to all Americans, because not everyone in this nation falls in this category. The reason I come to this conclusion is that there are a few that refuse to take advantage of educational opportunities and do not have any choice but to take whatever job is available to them. Sometimes these are the jobs that illegal immigrants have. Although I sometimes wonder why people do not want to earn an honest day's work and would rather live off the "politician's hand-outs," most commonly known as social programs. This is the reason they make it easier for those that claim that illegal immigrants only take jobs Americans do not want. The only people that should not be working in this country are the mentally or physically disabled who legitimately cannot; everyone else should earn a living. This is another factor that illegal immigrants have to be given credit for; they will take advantage of anything and everything that is available to them. They all want to be the best in whatever they do or is available to them.

The last time I read some articles in criminology, illegal immigrant's crimes of every type have increased in this country at a rapid pace. It is especially in the larger states in the northeast, west, and all those with a southern border. Again, not all illegal immigrants are criminals; the majority is hard working and just looking for the opportunity of a better life. The only problem is that a few make the headlines in the newspapers and make it harder for the rest of the immigrants. The crimes, ranging from kidnapping; drug trafficking; murders; robberies; drunk driving; rapes, and homicides, have been on the rise. We have enough criminals of our own that we have to house, feed, and educate. Now our taxes are going to be wasted with these antisocials from the illegal immigrants, to add to the list of burdens on our society. Gang activities, from illegal immigrants have grown at an alarming rate and, continue to rise. By not knowing the language and the fact that employment and housing is non-existent, too many illegal immigrants turn to criminal activities. Illegal drug trafficking is the only reported crime, but lately it accompanies kidnapping and murders. The media do not report these incidents but I will discuss this in another chapter.

You might be wondering why the problem of illegal immigration affects your American Dream. Please remember, one of the basic four of education, analyzing and math; because it affects employment, your identity, safety, criminal activities, education, your children's health and welfare, the election of government officials and your taxes spent in social programs for those not entitled too. They affect your employment because in this rough economy, you will have to be in the unemployment line for a longer period because of lack of employment. If you and your family are in need, you will take any job until things get better with the present economy. You do not know who is presently utilizing your social security number for employment or obtaining credit cards, which affect your social security benefits and credit rating by obtaining credit cards or loans with your information and failing to repay these debts. How many times have you heard on the news of murders, home invasions or vehicular homicides committed by illegals with our judicial system giving them a pass [and no penalties], because of their immigration status? We complain that our educational system is in shambles because of lack of funds, but this dual or special educational system contributes to failing the funding of our children's education. Our health, welfare, and that of children is affected because our politicians want to put a "band aid" on the health and medical care in the United States. The ones that are driving most of the cost of medical care are illegal immigrants that have no medical insurance and emergency rooms are the ones that cost the most in this country. It is documented that immigrants come to the "famous theme parks" in the State of Florida and overstay their tourist visas to obtain medical care, which is not available in their homeland or the cost is outrageous. They will get it free here, with a cost in the thousands of dollars at the expense of US taxpayers. This practice is not monitored by immigration agency officials, but happens on a routine basis. Additionally, part of the reason for high cost of medical care in the nation is their lack of documentation, which causes unscrupulous employers not to be able to provide medical insurance because of their status and abuse the system. This is another reason why these employers should be prosecuted to the full extent of the law. They are contributing to the astronomical cost of medical insurance in this nation. Our elected officials apparently live in a dream world, as they think that illegal immigrants will buy medical insurance to cover their expenses. If you can get free medical care at the emergency room, why should you pay for it and reduce the amount of money that you are sending home to your family? Because our federal government either, does not have the capabilities to verify false information of any type, or refuses to acknowledge or take action when known these illegal immigrants apply for social programs. Due to humanitarian reasons and a "golden heart" of the American people, sympathy takes over and they get away with everything. Enough is enough and we should demand our elected officials to find a solution to this problem. I am terribly sorry to put it this way, but if you have some "squatters" that invade your land, you will demand law enforcement to assist you in getting them out. You will not give an amnesty program to allow them to stay on your land and take over. If you think about it, this is what is going on in this nation and all because the politicians want to appease the Hispanic voters for their own agenda. It is time to protect our citizens and those enforcing the law against criminals in our borders. We should fight back with force, if necessary, for our own safety and freedom. We should not allow another American life to be taken away by illegal immigrants or criminals in our borders, especially if they are enforcing the laws of the land and protecting us. I never thought that our sovereignty was up for grabs, for sale or for politicians to play with it. We should practice what we preach and apply the freedom and democracy that we try to establish in other nations, in our own backyard. If you do not care about the issues that affect your family and the future of your children, just be silent. Turn the other way and take the "do nothing attitude". I am sure that you want something better for yourself and your family. It is time to voice your opinion and take some action by letting your elected officials know how you feel and to respect your wishes. After all, they are supposed to be working for us not for any political party, activist groups, or lobbyists in Washington. It is time to stop wanting to appease these groups in order to have an advantage in their thirst for power. You should demand "town hall" meetings with your elected officials in order to voice your opinions and the needs in your state. If your elected officials are deaf and do not listen, you have the weapon, your vote. Send him or her to a retirement home to give them time to think about it. Do not allow them to manipulate your voice or vote when it affects something as important as your life and that of your family.

ECONOMY

I do not claim to be an expert economist, but having a college education and plenty of common sense, I will render my opinion based on how this economy affects my family, budget, our lives, and me. I have and use my common sense and apply the basic four of education; read, write, analyze and math, which allows to make an educated analysis of the economical situation. The economy of this country has deteriorated in the last three decades. This has been because of the financial greed of those who run the financial market and institutions. Also, the thirst for power from politicians, who have passed terrible legislation in the interest of financial corporations instead of the American people. As a true American who loves this nation, I plea to the rest of the population to pull together and work hard in order for this economy to improve. Although our politicians in Washington have gotten us into this mess, let us hope that they are all successful for the betterment of the whole nation or else, we vote them out of office.

For starters, I always remember a Chinese proverb that my grandfather told me when I was a little kid and I quote: "If you do not know the rules of the game, do not play because if you lose, you cannot blame anybody but yourself." Perhaps I was not wise enough to adhere to some sound advice and fell victim to the stock market. Like many other Americans, I thought that with little knowledge I would be able to double or triple my hard-earned money for a rainy day. Nevertheless, "one of those brothers" played with my money and went bankrupt. It was enough for me and I wish others the best of luck because I would not allow the "same puppy" to nip my butt twice in a row. All I can say is that I wish them well in the Caribbean or Europe wherever they are, enjoying their good fortune, sipping cold daiquiris and laughing about fools like me. I do not regret anything because you are allowed to make mistakes in life, as long as you learn from your mistakes. If you commit the same mistake over and over again, then you must be a masochist or completely stupid. People do not understand that today, very few become multi millionaires unless they are born into money. You must have a fantastic entrepreneurial idea, incorporate it into the stock market, and find some investors or fools like me that are willing to take a chance on your idea. The only ones that become millionaires are the ones that run the market, investing firms and the stockbrokers that are gambling with your money. It is a shame, but where there is the human factor and money, greed overtakes the human behavior and fraud comes to mind. A good example is the few convictions of insider trading, to include politicians, yet nothing happens to the "big fish" and only the working people who lose their money. I feel sorry for those who have lost their life savings at the hands of some market's common crooks. The stock market goes up and down and your dividends of investments are minimal. Additionally, with the proposed tax increase in capital gains by politicians, investing in the stock market is not a great idea unless you have a fortune to invest. Investing nowadays in the stock market is no different from gambling or playing the lottery because you have the same chances of making it big. Sometimes it is safer to gamble or play the lottery because you are taking a chance by your own intuition and not on that of somebody that knows as much or as little as you do. The record of accomplishment that investing corporations, brokerage firms, and financial advisors have in the last two decades leaves a lot to be desired. All the fraud and abuse committed by unscrupulous individuals is disgraceful. My heart goes to those naïve individuals who, with the hope of making a lot of money, invest their life savings or retirement funds with a negative result because of these individuals. Additionally, with the tax laws, I think they are better off depositing their money in different banks where it is insured and sometimes make the same profit. As long as you diversify your funds in different banks, it is safer than the stock market. The days of making money in the market are over because when you have the same individuals managing the market, they become crooks and rob you blind. I repeat, just read, analyze, and figure out what has happened in the last three decades in the stock market. If you have money to spare or do not need it in your near future, put it in the stock market. However, if not, do not place your retirement or life savings in the stock market because it is not safe. In my opinion, the stock market is a long-term investment because of the instability that exists nowadays with the different corporations that you invest. Many will dispute this idea, but I tried and lost and those "experts" in the game have different opinions because they want you to invest your money in the stock market. The new way to get your money that some fall into is the new game where "eminent stock geniuses" have designed and sell internet programs to convert you into "a day trader." The only ones that become millionaires are the ones that sell you the computer program. I think it is good entertainment. It makes you feel good with a thought that you are investing and making some money in the market. I am willing to bet that day traders must seek other employment in order to make a living and pay their bills, because I do not think that day trading puts food on the table. The only way this is different is if you "day trade" in very large amounts; if you do, might as well go to the "big leagues" and go straight to Wall Street. By the way, these day traders are the ones that make the stock market less predictable because you do not really know what is going on. They affect the market because it shows that it is sky high positive in the opening session and bottom low negative by closing or vice versa. You have millions of "amateur stock brokers" all over the United States practicing this system. If you want or are looking for good entertainment, want to feel good, and are willing to pay hundreds of dollars for a computer program, then go to one of those seminars that are listed as infomercials on television and become a "day trader." My suggestion to all Americans is not to place your money under the mattress, but if you want to enjoy and play with your money, take a cruise or fly to another continent. Enjoy your hard-earned money while you can and have positive memories of how your money is spent or disappears. Do not gamble in the stock market until it is fixed, regulated, and controlled. If someone takes your money, let him or her rot in jail for the rest of his or her life. Let them suffer the same way you will suffer without your money. The good thing about the stock market is that by the "art of magic," it usually corrects itself and levels out.

The greatest detriment to the United States economy was the housing market. As a part of the American Dream, every family wants to own a house with a white picket fence. This dream can be achieved as long as you meet the requirement to make a twenty percent down payment and are able to make the mortgage payments for the next number of years. This will give you pride and comply with your commitment to hold on to the house and forget the federal government bailing you out of debt or providing any handouts. Thanks to "genius" politicians, compounded with unscrupulous financial institutions, officials were the cause of the dismay of the global economy. The greed of these individuals, by putting into practice the buying and selling of toxic accounts, created the worst financial chaos of all times. Certain politicians are as guilty because they sold the idea that, everyone, like everything else had the right to own a home, even when they could not afford it. I do not feel a bit sorry for all those individuals that got into mortgages that they could not afford. Remember the basic four of education; read, write, analyze and math. If all these individuals had mastered these skills, this would not have happened. They do not have anyone to blame but themselves, for being just plain greedy dummies. Instead of trying to add the unused money back into programs that are in dire need of funds (such as Social Security), politicians choose to filter out that money to fund their personal pet projects. I am sure that my grandchildren know that before you buy something you have to figure out if you can afford it, read anything you sign, analyze the terms of the contract, and use your math skills to figure out the payments. I am completely convinced in the rules of life and the basis of the capitalistic system of this country, which are choices. When you make the right choice, you live a happy life, but if you make the wrong choice, you have to suffer the consequences. It is too common in our country not to accept responsibility for our mistakes or actions and always blame someone else. We also refuse to accept the word NO, when we cannot have what we want. Another golden rule of life is that everybody has wants, but we do not always get what we want because we can only get what we qualify or are able to afford. Like the Rolling Stones sang, you can't always get what you want. Financial institutions are as guilty as the politicians and individuals, because loan officials geared by greed of bonuses were approving loans to unqualified "blue collar" workers with loans for million dollar mansions. Politicians, in order or receive political support were putting pressure to financial institutions to approve these loans and passing the most moronic legislation. It is a fact of life that not everyone can afford to buy a house. If they do, they should be aware of their income and the mortgage commitment. Amazingly, the politicians got a pass for their actions, were pardoned by the American people, and as a prize, were re-elected. Something else that influenced the bursting of the housing bubble was all the real estate speculators that saw an opportunity to "flip" houses for a profit. I always believe in ignorance because we are not infallible but not in stupidity; all these people that bought houses that they could not afford and also the speculators that wanted to make fast money should suffer the consequences and take their losses. The excuse that it diminishes the value of other houses in a community is nothing but an excuse. Politicians are trying to cover their tracks and provide government assistance with taxpayer's money, to appease their constituents. If I do not fall in this category, why should I pay for the stupidity of those individuals and suffer consequences for doing things correctly. With the excuse that this housing market fiasco is going to worsen the economy, now the government is even thinking of becoming the greatest real estate broker of the world. If the government is going to bailout the dummies for not upholding their commitments, what about giving a bonus to those who did the right thing. Those who did not default on their loans and continue to keep up with their commitments. I am convinced that we have reached a point in our lives that we must force individuals to accept responsibilities for their actions and suffer the consequences of their mistakes and bad choices.

The financial institutions in this country have tightened the availability of credit for small businesses and the line of credit for every individual. Although they have been guilty in the economy's debacle, now they are penalizing every American for their greed and unscrupulous practices. They are guilty as charged because of approving real estate loans to unqualified individuals. Furthermore, they "cooked the books" in order to sell to each other "toxic/sick" loan documents in order to appear solvent and continue their bad banking practices. What is completely sickening is that there were no regulations to control these practices and in the end, politicians started blaming each other for lack of regulations and oversight. Politicians of all parties and every branch of the government are guilty as charged. They should all remember, when you point a finger at someone-there are three pointing back at you. These unethical practices have been going for decades, and finally the housing bubble burst. They could no longer continue these practices so some of the institutions went bankrupt and they were in need of government assistance in order to slow down the total collapse of the economy. A depressing situation is that with all the government assistance, [I refuse to use dirty words and I do not like to use the "bailout" word] they continue to pay themselves millions in bonuses and spend millions in conventions for their top executives. What is sad is that financial institutions claim that they were forced by the government to take the assistance even if they did not need it. Anger is the only thing that is felt by most Americans, because the same people that were making these unscrupulous financial practices are the ones now in charge of handling the United States Treasury, which is completely unbelievable. Now that the financial institutions want to pay all these billions in assistance back, the government refuses to take it, because they do not want to release control of the institutions. Furthermore, the taxpayers own part of these institutions because they are using our tax money. Yet they continue to abuse common citizens with "funny practices" for interest rates on loans and credit cards. This is double jeopardy for the common citizens because they use your money to make twice their money. Now the common excuse is that they have to pay those high bonuses to their executives because they cannot find qualified individuals to fill these positions. I would be willing to bet my life that if you give these positions to small business entrepreneurs, they will do the same or a better job for less money. Small business individuals have been able to manage their business for years, being successful without "cooking the books" and they have more common sense than these idiots do. If these high paid executives would use their abilities and skills for something good, it would warrant their salaries. The problem is that their greed makes them look for ways to swindle investors; they think its okay, until they are caught. Furthermore, it is not hard to find a common criminal on every corner of a big city in the United States and maybe it will be cheaper than millions. We should remember that behind every successful executive, there is a fantastic administrative assistant or executive secretary that knows more about the institution than the executive officer does. Success usually depends on the people that surround the person in charge or the head of the institution. Sorry, but no matter how you dress a crook, he, or she is still a crook and should receive the same punishment. What is sad and confusing is the apathy demonstrated by shareholders, who continue to be silent and do not express their disgust with the practices of the executive officers of these institutions. I have not been able to figure out the position of shareholders and investors to date, that allow these executive officers to pay themselves these millions of dollars in bonuses. Although, it is better for the shareholders to intervene in this problem, rather than naming a government official to regulate all pay and allowances for private corporations because you never know how far they will go before it stops. It makes me wonder they do not care, but are trying to hide their fortune and just role it over to avoid paying any taxes to the federal government.

Our elected officials have been entrusted, by the people, with the power to oversee problems of this nature. Their main mission is to pass regulatory legislation to avoid these types of dismay to the nation's economy. Instead of providing congressional oversight, they look after each other guilt free. It seems that they are part of the organized crime group and they receive "sweetheart deals" or special favors from the financial institutions, inside trading, and political support in their thirst for power. It is so shameful that these elected officials, due to personal interest, legislate in favor of the institutions instead of the taxpayers that voted them into power. It is known that they even have family members working in these institutions or the market and they do not consider this unethical or a conflict of interest. Furthermore, they will only take or initiate corrective action when they are in fear their "elected seat" is in jeopardy. The problem is that not all elected officials caught in unethical practices are investigated. So many of them have skeletons hidden in their closets, that they won't have any congressional hearings or punish these individuals for fear their secret will come to light. It seems that the congressional ethics committee is one of the greatest jokes because all their investigations end in nothing and just make a "show investigation" to appease the American people, as if they are actually doing something. I will discuss in more details the failure of our government in a later chapter.

I fully understand that in our capitalistic system, credit is the most important commodity that we have. We have reached a time in our lives where we should start tightening our belts and use the principle of "pay as you go." I hope that the idiots that we send to Washington will do the same with our tax money and government expenditures. I also understand that with the economy the way it is and the percentage of unemployment sky high every month, we have the tendency to abuse our credit and our credit cards. We are so used to "charging" to buy everything we want. We should start to think, read the small print and analyze on our credit card agreements and use what we learned in math to figure the rate of interest that the bank hoodlums are charging us. They should not do this practice because "we the people" own most of the banks now, but they need their bonus and convention monies. I think that this is like being tried twice for the same crime, but our legislative and executive branches of government do not give a hoot about the people, they only care about their own agenda. We should adhere to the advice of our grandparents and save for what we want unless it is for necessities. There is an old saying that you cover yourself as far as your blanket will go; if you pull too much, some part of your body will be cold. If you want something so bad that you cannot live without it, go to the store or dealer and look at it every time you have the urge. This will give you a bigger incentive to save until you can get it. That means that if we are not careful, we will fall in the "take away from Peter to pay Paul" syndrome. We will always be in debt, pay only interest to our debts without subtracting parts of the principal and the financial companies will be taking advantage of you. Stores, banks, and financial institutions are in heaven when you have a wallet or purse full of credit cards from every possible store or financial institution. This applies to purchasing major appliances and new vehicles. Keeping up with the Jones' can no longer be the mindset in today's economy. If you cannot go to the Super Bowl, a 60' plasma TV is not going to change the outcome of the game or put you in the stadium where the game is played. The same applies to cars, if you drive your old Japanese car to work, a new German car is not going to get you out of traffic or get you to work earlier or faster. If you cannot afford something, be content with what you have and count your blessings. Maybe if you save enough and work hard, some day you will have the best things in life; committing yourself, through credit, for all these debts is not worth it and in the long run will hurt you. You should live within your means and pay as you go to avoid complications in your life. Vanity is the worst thing that a person can have because you do not have to keep with anyone but yourself. All vanity does is get you in trouble and a whole lot of debt because it becomes an addiction. A person that pays as they go is an extremely happy person. Moreover, you cannot take it with you when you die.

Our tax code is another of the "highway robberies" by the federal government that must be examined and revised. The present tax code is so complicated that not even Internal Revenue workers understand them and there is no uniform system to apply to delinquent citizens or to those citizens or corporations that under pay their taxes. I consider it an unfair system because the middle class, or the hard working population, are the only ones that actually pay their fair share of taxes based on their income. Those that are in the "privileged class" pay after they deduct and claim all the "loopholes" allowable by the law. The only ones that are gaining with the present tax laws are those who are "leeches" of the federal government's social programs or those that for unknown reasons do not pay taxes at all. This part of the population is the one that benefits the most of the two higher paying classes because they receive more assistance from the federal government. Amazingly, our taxes are for paying for schools; help with infrastructure, federal government services, some healthcare, welfare, and the organized crime of Washington. However, for those of us that do not receive any benefits of this nature, we are losing in this game because our money is going down the toilet. Politicians have plans to increase or change the tax code to defray the cost of new government programs. At the rate that we are going, we will soon have to receive ration cards from the federal government in the form of welfare because we will not be able to afford our necessities with the wages we earn.

Will the system change to make the tax codes and laws more equitable? Not as long as it is left to elected officials, because they will lessen the funds to sponsor their pork/pet projects, their humongous expense accounts and trips around the world at our expense. It is understandable that as citizens of this nation, we should pay taxes for the defense, education, part of the inner structure and certain regulatory departments of the federal government and for the health and welfare of the citizens. I understand that Americans have "hearts of gold" and this is a super power nation, but we are not the keepers of the world. After studying the monies that the United States donates to other nations of the world through the United Nations, it is unbelievable because it should be more equitable with other nations. Sometimes our politicians should take care of home first and then help the rest of the world. Especially when we are helping nations that hate our system of government, standard of living and it all goes to a corrupt few in a government that often is not even a democracy. We have to stop buying allies with our tax money, especially now that our economy is in shambles.

If you figure out what we pay in income taxes, federal and state tax on the fuel we consume, state tax and sales tax every time we use one dollar that we earn that is more than enough taxes. This does not include the taxes on our basic needs such as water and sewage, electricity, telephone and trash collection are all added to our dollar earned. It will not surprise me that with the new green initiative of the federal government, we will have to pay for the air we breathe because they have started with what we exhale. By the time, we finish paying all the taxes to the federal and state governments, plus our basic needs, out of the dollar we earned we have left about ten cents. We should realize that higher taxes to the workers, small businesses, and industries would end our employment because small businesses and employers can no longer survive this practice. When will it stop and what can we do about it? I will let you decide. We are getting close to the point of no return because we continue to be silent and assume the "I don't care" attitude.

This present tax code's affect on corporations and industries, has resulted in major corporations outsourcing their services and production to other countries, which provide tax exemptions or lower taxes. Additionally, they try to find cheaper labor costs due to many organized labor unions which increase the costs of labor that are passed on to the consumer. In this economy, we must always remember that in a capitalistic system, an entrepreneur invests and risks his or her capital for a profit and not to share with the government or less advantaged people. Consequently, we cannot apply the "Robin Hood" theory that you can take away from the successful or rich and give to the poor. If you do, the rich are going to take their money and run. That is why outsourcing complicates the overall population of this nation, because it diminishes the job opportunities in this nation and increases the taxes for those few that work, because the government needs the necessary funds to function. Additionally, the lower tariffs imposed on the major countries that trade with our nation complicates our Gross National Product (GNP) and our Gross Domestic Product (GDP) because it subtracts from the nation's income. When we start spending more than what we earn or more than our income, we should use the dirty word NO or STOP. When we reach this point in our government, we have the option to borrow more money from other nations or are forced to print more money. This practice of printing more money by the federal government will result in the devaluation of the United States dollar and creates a state of inflation in the nation. This is worse than the recession (soon to become a depression) we are living now, because it will have a greater effect on all consumers and the financial system. At this rate, with the nation borrowing money from other competitive nations, we will end up like a third world country because we will not be able to sustain the expenditures of social programs, size of the government and overall cost of the functions of this nation. When you spend more than what you earn, you end up with chaos because nobody will buy our debt, our federal reserve is getting slimmer, and our dollar is not worth its full value anymore (which is now about sixty-five cents).

The present administration is no different from prior administrations, by trying to pass legislation as soon as possible, for fear of losing the majority in congress. I make the distinction that there is no difference between politicians of either parties because they all subscribe to this practice when they are the majority in power. I am perplexed and cannot understand how our elected officials can pass legislation without reading what they are voting for and the only ones that know what is in the legislation are their staffers. Maybe the problem is that our elected officials either cannot read, do not care what they are voting for, their political party is more important that their constituents, they are voting in favor of lobbyist or special interest groups or they are just plain senile and cannot perform their duties as representatives of the American people. History shows that the founding fathers' idea was to have a balance of power to avoid these types of situations in our government. They could foresee that when there was no balance of power, the nation was in danger of collapsing. The American people are so tired of politicians and the system, that they will vote and try anything in order to find a solution to a failing federal government. The previous administration got us into a myriad of problems here at home and overseas, which created a deep hole in our economy, difficult to get out of. The only problem with the present administration is that in their short time in power, they started with "big shovels" and have dug us deeper into spending and deficit. With the excuse that they inherited a bad economy, deficit, and a financial system in shambles, they have been very successful in making it worse within a short period. By controlling the Executive and Legislative branches, they are passing or trying to pass legislation at the speed of lightning, without fully allowing the American people to be aware of what they are getting us into. This has affected most of the American people because most of the population is unemployed. Suffering the most is the middle class. Under the guise of saving the economy, they have been able to appease a great number of political supporters and "putting the screws" to the majority. Presently there is no true prediction of when this economy is going get better and until this happens, the middle class continues to suffer and possibly pay higher taxes. It does not pay to be successful in this nation because if you are successful, you are required to pay higher taxes to support the unsuccessful. With the excuse of "leveling the playing field," politicians will apply the "Robin Hood" principle and allow them to piggyback on the successful. Though the legislation that was intended to save the economy, the famous "bailout," has resulted in negative improvement of the economy and been utilized for pet projects which do not help anyone except a select few? If there is another "bailout" as planned by many politicians, we have no choice but to rebel, call, and send electronic mail to our representatives until the system explodes. If you are able to imagine how many zeros a billion dollars has, multiply by ten and you will figure out where our debt is. This will not end because they continue to pass legislation that will place us in a deeper hole, with more debt. Countries are afraid to lend us more money and want to start receiving payment on what we owe. What the federal government gets involved in does not come free, nor is it cheap. It seems that the blind is leading the blind in Washington and nobody really knows what they are doing. If they do not find a crystal ball or a "voodoo doctor," they will continue with their trial and error in Washington. What is a shame is that apparently the stock market, what they were blaming for a bad economy, is slowly correcting itself. With this suffering, to the American people, comes a big lesson which is that we have to be very careful what we wish for, or who and what we vote. We should remember that not everything that shines is gold and we have to be very careful with the false promises of politicians.

I will try to make a synopsis of something very special, which is family Economy 101, and demonstrate how it affects our lives in the United States of America. Entrepreneurs invest and risk capital with the ultimate goal of making a profit. Our capitalistic system requires entrepreneurs and small businesses, which are the greater providers of employment in the nation, in order to function. With the new taxation laws and the new government initiative of health care, it will destroy all small businesses. I have made an analysis based on the "Bell Curve" grading principal. Using this grading system, you can see that on the bottom spectrum of the curve is the population number that pays the minimum or no tax at all. The top spectrum of the curve is the population that pays the maximum percentage of taxes, but the population is reduced as it escalates in income. The bulk of tax payers are in the middle, which is the greatest majority of the population. This population in the middle of the "Bell Curve" is the one that finances the majority of government programs and expenditures. Conveniently, the promise of reducing taxes to the majority of the population is bogus because taxes will remain the same for those that pay no taxes and a "tax break" of two thousand dollars annually will not be of great help for a family of four. Additionally, politicians fall in the middle of the curve as their salaries fall below the magic number of two hundred and fifty thousands, which is no surprise. The bulk of their income is "tax free" because it is based on the expense accounts they receive and that run into the millions per politician. The others that get the short end of the stick are small business owners because on paper, they fall above the magic number, but in actuality, their income is less. Contrary to what politicians preach, increased taxes over the amount of two hundred fifty thousand dollars will force small business to either go bankrupt or cease operating. The way small businesses operate is dependent upon contracts that will not allow them to receive money or funds up to six months or more in advance, but payroll and benefits continue until they receive the actual payment of funds after completion of a contract. On the books, it reflects this income but in actuality, monies are not in the bank even though taxes must be paid as recorded by accountants. The new taxation laws and health initiative will result in layoffs of a great number of employees and loss of jobs, because small business owners cannot sustain these initiatives. Politicians do not understand this concept because most of them have not even taken care of a family budget. This initiative creates a "domino effect" because less people employed are fewer taxes for the government, less taxes from the small businesses, increased unemployment, and worsened economy. Additionally, with the new initiative to appease big labor unions because of their political support, it will stop entrepreneurs from investing their time and money in any business adventure. The "blank card" initiative by politicians, forcing corporations to accept workers unions, will ensure that they outsource their businesses overseas. You do not invest your capital to pass on your profits to workers unions in salaries and lifetime benefits. You can provide a fair wage for any type of work, but you cannot become prisoners of labor unions, which are the reason why many corporations and small businesses go bankrupt upon accepting the terms of these workers unions. Good examples are the auto and steel industries that became dependent on government assistance in order to continue in operation with no assurance of success, no matter what program politicians "invent" to insure their success. This government assistance would be better utilized by small businesses in the continental United States and provide more jobs than financial institutions and the auto industries. Now, the assistance provided to financial institutions has been in vain because they do not provide credit to the people who need it. .

You will ask why the economy affects your American Dream, but if you think how hard, you work, if you have a job, and where are you planning to go and what are your dreams for the future. The harder you work, the less you have for yourself, your family, and the slimmer the chances of your dreams coming true. This is the nation of opportunity and prosperity, but at the rate we are going, all we are doing is work to pay taxes and our debts and no more. This is the land in which every man and woman has the opportunity to work hard and be successful. This is the land of choices and when you make the right choice, you live a happy life, but if you make the wrong choice, you must suffer the consequences. Enough is enough and it should stop because we should not have to take care of those who make the wrong choices or do not want to take advantages of the opportunities like every other American. We should turn the page and start with a clean slate. Force those so called disadvantaged to take charge and responsibilities of their lives. We should not be paying for things that happened before our times and be indebted for the rest of our lives. Right now, our children and grandchildren will be paying for something that happened when they were not around, consequently why should the unborn pay for these atrocities. If the politicians want to "level the playing field," let it be leveled for every American, not only for a few. My children and grandchildren deserve the same opportunities and as long as I am alive, I will demand it from elected officials and you should do the same. If you are able to save some and take the chance to invest your savings, you are taking a great chance that what you invest in will go under, or the government will take over. What is sad is that if the government takes over, your dividends will be less than what you invested because the Bankruptcy Court will give the benefit as payback for political favors or support, to unions, failed corporations and use your taxes as assistance. This seems to be double jeopardy because you lose twice by trying to get ahead and investing your life savings and they will use your taxes to assist these failed corporations in the name of saving the economy. It is time to tighten our belts and watch our expenditures. Ignore the federal government when the politicians urge us to spend more to boost the economy. If the government does not curve their spending, we should or we will wind up at the soup line and no politician will care what happens to us. I urge you to think twice before you spend your money on frivolous things and have at least six months of savings to cover your basic expenditures in case you lose your job or are unable to find employment. Think twice before you get in over your head and try to avoid playing the investment game without having any knowledge of how to do it. A word of caution, be careful with whom you entrust your money to invest for you because you might "cry tears of blood," or be left with a heart full of sorrow. Your first responsibility is to yourself and your family because "charity" starts at home and you always give as much as you can, but within your limitations. The greatest lesson that we, the American people, have to learn is that no matter what political party you are affiliated with, you should never allow this complete control of power. There should always be a balance, in the hopes of keeping honest our elected officials so they will legislate in the best interest of their constituents and not in favor of party lines, special interest, personal agenda, or corporate lobbyist groups. This was why our founding fathers developed our form of government, into three branches, to maintain balance of power. If we want to get rid of certain politicians, we can always do it in a balanced way without losing our heads in the name of "change." I always say that we are allowed to make mistakes. As long as we learn from our mistakes and avoid committing the same mistake twice. We should not loose our heads and out of desperation allow politicians to manipulate us with their false promises. Be levelheaded, do the right thing when casting your vote, and be extremely careful whom you re-elect for another term in office. Examine their voting record and legislation that this individual has been a part of or initiated. You have some politicians that go to Washington to "vegetate," make money and waste your money. They earn a government pension and enjoy the benefits of being in Congress with all the added pack of "goodies" that go with the position of an elected official.

MEDIA

The media, written, spoken, video or internet are the most efficient way to influence the opinion of the American people. Although they have all the rights in this nation to express their opinion, because the United States Constitution grants them the freedom of speech and freedom of the press, they should make a public disclosure of their political position or ideology. It is sad and pathetic where journalism has gone in the past three decades. A few commentators, in the name of journalism, express their opinions disguised as the news or truth. True journalism stopped when Mr. Walter Cronkite retired from reporting the evening news. It died when this great journalist passed away. My utmost respect goes to his memory and the same to his surviving family members. It seems that through the name of journalistic media, all newspaper editors, television anchors, or reporters, internet bloggers and radio broadcasters, left and right, have turned news into paid political activists for both major political parties. It has gotten to the point that all they report is gossip, political attacks and vicious stories of political adversaries; that is sickening. This started in the 1990s and I hope it stops soon. All this does is to cause Americans to lose respect for journalism and those politicians they support. Maybe this is the reason why newspapers are going bankrupt and television stations lose their ratings-people get tired of these "school yard" fights. The American people have stopped buying or reading newspapers because of the political bias of journalists and editors.

Up until 1980, it was a pleasure to read a newspaper at breakfast, on the way to work, at your lunch break at the office or to listen to all television stations at 6 PM for the news. There were respectful news anchors and reporters that reported the actual news and you could "take it to the bank" because you knew it was the truth. As a matter of entertainment, I sit in front of the television set and flip channels to see which station tries to outdo the other one with their opinions and personal attacks, which is not necessarily true. It has gotten so bad that they report what is convenient to their agenda and ignore the truth because it will hurt their political support. It reminds me of a three-ring circus because you can enjoy and laugh at the three different shows at the same time. They report the same event with different versions, according to their political agenda. It is interesting how the same event or news can have multiple versions of the occurrence when it happened at the same day, time, and place. It seems that all have a hidden agenda in their programming and everything is edited in accordance with the desires of the chief executive officer's political views. A person with a high level of education and intelligence can see their bias, especially when they promote their hidden agenda towards a certain politician or political party. What is important to highlight is that this is an investment on their part because, once their candidate of choice wins any governmental position, they can collect the political favor for which they have worked so hard. These political favors are collected and not seen by the average American because the networks are like "octopuses" and they have their tentacles in other types are businesses. They utilize strong lobbyists to fight for their causes and have legislation passed in their favor to enhance their other businesses.

The side show of these newscasters and their programs are their guests, which support their agenda. Some are their newspaper counterparts, failed radio or television hosts, their assigned investigative reporters who collect all the gossip or frustrated politicians who have been replaced by voters in their elected position. Additionally, they have as guests those frustrated politicians who have tried to run for an elected position but have been unable to convince voters to elect them. The "icing on the cake" is those guests who are self-proclaimed political analyst or strategist, military analyst and expert in any topic. It is amazing that in America we love titles and are willing to add anything to a résumé and with good connections, we are selected to make a fool of ourselves. The political analysts or strategists are usually campaigning volunteers who distribute flyers, beg for contributions, or are plain "gophers" for a politician. I compare these groups of individuals to parrots, because they repeat the same talking points repeatedly no matter what you ask or what the debate is. They keep repeating the script that they were given by higher ups, like telemarketers who have a basic script and a rebuttal when challenged. A few of the military experts have not even worn a "boy scout" uniform, been in the military or been close to any type of conflict or war and don't even know the military base closest to them. The biggest joke is that the closest conflict they have had is with their siblings, spouse or in a high crime area in a big city. They usually have the audacity to criticize men and women in uniform or true military experts. These military experts haven't even have served this nation in any capacity, but that of a congressional "gopher" making copies of documents or taking documents from one office to another. They should kiss the ground where they are standing because, thanks to the sacrifice of those in uniform whom they criticize, they have the opportunities that they do. I doubt much the qualifications of the political analysts or strategists, because it takes a special kind of individual to lower him or herself so low as to earn their way by being in the right place at the right time, rubbing elbows of influential people and not by their own merits. I guess this is the good American way in politics and everything counts or goes. One thing that irks me about those military analysts is they base their criticism on what they have heard or read in a book of their convenience, not by personal experiences. Military strategy, behavior and tactics are not learned by reading a book, but by hands on and personal experiences. Letters, words, and sentences do not shoot bullets from a library in college or The Library of Congress in Washington.

What is sad about this situation is that the media targets those individuals in the population who were absent and missed two of the basic four during the early years of their basic education or home training. These targeted individuals do not like to read or do not understand what they read. Consequently, they dedicate most of their time to watching television and what some "respectable" newscasters interpreted as the truth. They have not been trained to analyze and digest the pros and cons, the hidden agenda or the bias propaganda of the media. This is the process of "brainwashing" individuals because the more you repeat the same information, lies, or an opinion, it sounds more, and more like the truth to most of the less educated population. Catchy phrases like "unfair war," "all for change," "inherited this" and "tax cut for" once repeated repeatedly, resonates in the brain of people, and is believed by most Americans. Additionally, some "comedy shows" utilize the networks to plug their political bias, in the name of comedy. This is also sad because their target audience is seniors, less educated minorities or young men and women in college alike. This is compounded with professors with the same agenda. Colleges will turn into infomercials on television, very effective and easy prey, for politicians and people in the media. When a number of college students are interviewed on current political events, they will repeat verbatim the same information that is played by infomercials on television. Amazingly, sometimes they quote the person by name, and if he or she says it, it must be true. These are the same group of individuals that are targeted through the internet by the "bloggers" because they are more knowledgeable in computers. They are given information they want to hear, such as, advantages in support to defray their educational costs and free college education, which are completely out of this world. If they stop and think, it is virtually impossible for a student to receive a free college education, because of the cost and number of students in this nation. These "bloggers" know the right "buttons" to push to gain political support. It is sad because these are our most brilliant minds in the United States of America. It is amazing that individuals with this educational level will not "weed out" the truth from what is political banter to gain their vote.

Seniors are part of the population that is targeted the most, because they are the largest voting block in the nation. The media's tactic is to scare them that their Social Security and Medicare benefits are going to either be cut or taken away by one party or the other. They do not understand that these benefits cannot be taken away from them and the only way this will happen is if the systems go broke. Something that is very possible because of the "shifting" of funds by politicians from one agency to another. Not repaying these funds is what is driving these benefits to the pits and the life expectancy of the agency to been shortened by many years. Both political parties are guilty of this practice because both parties have been doing it for years. The ones that are not going to see any benefits are the younger than fifty group. By the time they become eligible, benefits will be exhausted. Additionally, seniors have a great interest in tax issues because most live on a limited income, which barely covers their monthly medical and basic necessities or because of poor health, they take away from "Peter to pay Paul." Last topic that seniors worry about is not allowing them to cast their vote for the candidate or party of their choice. Seniors are easy prey for the media, from the left and right, who take advantage repeating catchy phrases to the point they start to believe what they hear. This should be outlawed, but our politicians make the laws and this would be to their disadvantage. The party with more funds is the most effective one is scaring the senior population.

The last groups target by the media are the less educated and minorities. This is very sad because these two groups, unfortunately, do not know better. These groups are those that are high school dropouts, unemployed because of lack of skills, receiving public assistance or products of social programs. Others that fall in this category are those legal immigrants that have language barriers and are at the mercy of the federal government for all types of assistance. These two groups are the most vulnerable, because they are desperate for any type of change or shift in the governmental power to improve their standard of living. Most of these individuals have been left behind generation after generation by society. Although there are opportunities for everyone in this nation, they have the tendency to make the wrong choices time after time. Sometimes it makes you wonder if politicians want them to be in this state, in order to continue with their false promises and lure them as an easy vote for their political party. "They have been receiving the fish to eat for so many years, but have not been taught how to fish." They are completely dependent on the federal government for their survival. This most likely will not change because it is not in the best interest of politicians in Washington.

Newspapers have a little less influence on the targeted population because it seems that the number of people that buy and read newspapers has diminished at a rapid pace in the last two decades. Newspapers are very selective, depending on their political agenda, in what they place in their front pages as breaking news. If it favors their agenda, they place on the front page in large bold letters, but if not, you will see this news on page twenty in minute letters. The same applies to editorials because the "journalists" are no better than the commentators on television that report what they want and write things adjusting them to their agenda or opinion. Let it be clear that this applies to newspapers in which the proprietors and stockholders political ideology is to the left or right. What is comical is that most commentators in television quote a few of these newspapers as if the information they print is written in stone. Usually journalists from these newspapers are also guests on television programs. The newspaper industry is going down the tubes not only because of their political agenda, but also because of the growing number of bloggers and news sites on the internet.

I have not been able to decide which is the most unethical, vicious, or vile, the radio, or the internet. The reason that it is so hard to decide is, that the right wing's radio has more listeners and extremely vicious. The left has the most internet bloggers and very unethical and vile. This applies to both parties because they have the tendency to attack their rivals in politics, like wild animals destroying prey. Something very sad about these attacks is that they not only attack the candidates, but also the family regardless of age or gender. This is what gives "dirty politics" its name. They do not engage in debate of the issues or policies, but in personal attacks of family, friends, and associates. It is amazing where they can dig for so much dirt, but it is understandable why good men and women do not run for office or do not get involved in politics. This non-stop mission has the backing of multi millionaires who support and finance the campaigns of the politicians and parties of their choice. These are individuals or corporations with unlimited funds that are making an investment in a given candidate or party, for political advantage in their own interest. These well-managed teams of investigators and attorneys consider themselves above the law. This practice cannot be stopped because the politicians in the major governing party initiate it. This will also continue through the tenure of the political party in power, because politicians never stop campaigning and will start to attack and dig dirt on any possible rival. They also read daily polls on the status of their candidate to manage their attack plan. This is something equal to the military tactics of search and destroy. Attack your enemy or opponent before they are able to attack you and do harm. This is like the old saying that whoever hits first, wins the fight.

This is where I add humor. It is comedy to me because I am a registered voter with no party affiliation and have no ties to any political ideology. I vote on issues, regardless of the party of the candidate and do not get my pom-poms out to give hurrahs to any political party. During the campaign period, the "alphabet" television stations, which support the left, praise how the activist organizations were organizing to register voters, often committing voter fraud, in favor of the party in power. Additionally, the politicians in power were gloating. Smiling from ear to ear about this practice and were proud that their main candidate was the number one organizer. The "animal" television station, which supports the right, was furious and tried to bring this to the attention of the American people. The funny part of the equation is that now that the party in power is trying to pass a very sensitive legislation, they are accusing the other party of the same practice. The roles have reversed and the "alphabet" television stations are condemning this practice and the "animal" television station praises the practice. I find this humorous because of the hypocrisy involved in the process. When it is convenient, you approve and if not, you condemn the practice. Secondly, with all do respect to women, I have found that the most vicious personnel on both sides of the spectrum are females. As a form of entertainment, I switch television channels periodically to listen to the expert commentators from the left and right and come to my own conclusion. The "alphabet" and "animal" television stations, they have a great number of females who have been failures in their own television or radio talk shows, but have become television's self-proclaimed political analysts or strategist. These rehashed political failures, have been denied, or, were looking for positions in the political party of power. Their main mission is to find as much dirt or twist the truth to their advantage, to try to convince members of either party of current issues in the news. Again, I find it comical because they are convinced that they are achieving their goal, when in reality what they are doing is insulting the degree of intelligence of the American people. They do not realize that the American people are past this stage in their lives and not "buying" this nonsense, because we are smarter than the credit given by the media. What I suggest to the television networks is to start a daily show on prime time with the name of "piranhas versus barracudas" or "hyenas versus coyotes" and this will give them a better rating than what they have and will be more entertaining to the American people. I understand that this might not be hilarious to many Americans, because they are registered as a voter for one of the political parties. The lesson to learn here is, that it is better not to support or have any party affiliation, but vote according to issues regardless of the candidate's party's ideology. You should not lose your temper, do not be violent in any form. Be civil and conduct yourself properly, be respectful and you will be respected. You can allow your blood pressure to go sky high, but very calmly take notes for the next election cycle. This is the good news about the life span of a politician. In Congress, you have two years to get rid of them and find someone that has your best interest in mind and will represent you. If this does not happens, you have the opportunity to do it again and continue with the change until you find a candidate that really listens, answers you calls or e-mails and will represent you in Washington. Change is in your hands, with the correct vote, every election cycle. Beware of the new Federal Communication Czar, who is going to silence, by new regulation, your party's voice in radio. Do not be surprised of what the party in power is going to do to take another one of your rights – freedom of speech.

The media, newspaper, radio, television and internet, are some of the most influential factors that affect your American Dream. The reason why it is very influential is that it affects the way you elect your government officials, who are the ones that dictate the route the country is going. They have the tendency to gear the population to cast a ballot based on their "hearts" and not with their brain. They put out information, which is, not necessarily true, but the opinion of another person. By repetition, the population registers it as the truth because the "broadcasting celebrities," compounded with their "expert" guest, are very convincing. You must remember that these television hosts are very shrewd in the way they express their commentaries or opinions, with a hidden agenda geared to record in your brain the way they want you to vote. Sometimes you have individuals that do not have the ability to differentiate between the opinions of television commentators and the truth that their opinion is no better that your own opinion. They should remember the old saying that, "opinions are like belly buttons, and everybody has one." It is a shame because contrary to what many people in the media think, Americans are not dumb, but due to frustration or hopes for change, they are easily convinced. Most Americans are tired of the same lack of representation and politicians with their own agenda that they either do not vote or elect the first individual that tells them what they want to hear. You can come to your own conclusion on who is the correct candidate, who has your best interest or that of your family in mind. Once you allow these "celebrities" to gear you to vote a certain way, you are stuck with this individual for either two or four years. This is a long period of time for you and your family to suffer and you cannot take it back. Be smart. It is okay to listen to what everyone has to say, but you should digest all this data, analyze it, and come with your own conclusion prior to making a decision. It is better to make your own mistake, than be influenced by others and make a mistake on somebody else's opinion. You have heard that old saying that if it sounds too good to be true, it usually is. When politicians are elected and are in Washington, they are controlled by their party and will not legislate in your best interest. You make your own future with your vote by not electing or reelecting someone that has not done anything in your best interest or that of your family. You are smart and the only thing that you have to do is to remember two of the basics of your education and home training, read, analyze and finally, make your own decisions.

One thing, that the media of any type has, is that they do not allow the American people to turn the page on the history of this nation. When their candidate or party is behind in the polls or losing an election, they start throwing or pulling the racial card, female slurs or disqualifications and sexual preference of an individual. This is something the American people should be aware of in order to "weed out" the media's trash when presented and make your own decision on your selection of your candidate. You should never forget that both the left and the right are guilty of this practice. Remember to be smart and vote with your brain, not your heart, because you have more mental capacity than what they give you credit. You should never forget that most politicians and the media are convinced that the American people are dumb and uneducated, with no capacity to see through the "smoke screen" that they try to blow in front of your eyes. Many have openly expressed this sentiment during their commentaries on their programs. They practice a childish game of "dragging their blanket" to see who touches or steps on it, in order to pick an argument, criticize or bring down the opposite party – welcome to our great nation, because this is the American political system.

GOVERNMENT

The American governmental system is one of the best in the entire world. It is depressing that the founding fathers carefully established an almost perfect system of government, to avoid abuse of power or the situations that we have lived in the past three decades. It might be the establishment of only the two party systems, because the choices are limited and there is always control by one party or the other, without the check and balance intended. The system has deteriorated so much that it leads to corruption. It is time for the American people to take control and fix this problem. This also allows for deviation from or convenient interpretation of the United States Constitution, which dictates the law of the land. As a disclosure, I have been registered as a voter of each political party at one time or another and the disappointment has been so great, that now I am proud to say that I do not support in any form one political party. I cast my vote based on the issues, regardless of the candidate or party. I am glad that I have seen the light and gotten out of the syndrome of blindly supporting any given party, without analyzing the issues or what they present to the voting population, prior to casting my vote at the voting poll. You must remember that "trash" comes in different sizes, colors, shapes, or forms and you must disregard them when necessary.

I am perplexed and always refer to the four basics of education, because those who have not had the opportunity to achieve a higher level of education, by no fault of their own, are able to read, write, analyze and mathematically figure out that politics is the best "gig" in town. Politicians, with support of naïve voters, invest millions of dollars to be elected to a two or four-year term office and their federal salaries will not amount to a third of what they invest. I thought that it was because of thirst for power that politicians run for office and work so hard to be elected, but I have concluded that there is something else. I also gave them the benefit of the doubt because I thought that politicians wanted to make the difference and do something for the nation, but I guess I was wrong. There are many sweet deals from special interest, "pork" deals that involve relatives and close friends, and being above the law is the biggest incentive to run for office. Additionally, after researching and finding out that only in the House of Representatives they receive over one million dollars and the Senate close to two millions as an expense account, I figure that for starters this is a good investment. I hate to be a dirty thinker, but there is more to being elected to Congress and they receive other funds from corporations or lobbyist as payback for political favors as shown in their past legislation. Although there are only a few elected officials that have some of their family members as lobbyist, it makes you wonder and gives you a lot to ponder. Let it be clear that there are a small number that run for office for love of country, but this is few and far between. They are part of the great minority in Congress. Based on the fact that they make the laws and have to answer to no one, the Congressional Ethics Committee does what is expected from them – nothing. They only investigate the opposition. I have concluded that politics is the dirtiest career and most politicians are attorneys. I respect this profession, though, because it is not fair to generalize. I have come to the conclusion that most lawyers in politics and the federal government are crooked, think that they are above the law, that all Americans are dumb, and have taken the liberty to think for us, instead of represent us as demonstrated by their record. This applies to both political parties with no exception.

Our politicians have conveniently changed laws to accommodate their needs in every possible way and enhance their opportunities of being elected. For starters, there should be a limit to the campaign period of no more than six months. This is ample time to present their issues and ideas to their constituents and if they are convincing enough, the candidate will be elected into office. The idea behind this time limit in the campaign process is that it will reduce the political favors they become indebted with, through financial support. Consequently, if elected, they will legislate and fight for their constituents, instead of special interest. Elected officials should spend more time in Washington doing their job. Between returning to their district to campaign for re-election, or holiday and seasonal breaks, very little time is actually spent representing their constituents. This is not too much to ask, because political donations are tax deductable and should be able to be traced by the Internal Revenue Service. Additionally, there should be a limit to the amount of funds candidates are allowed to use in the process. All donations, regardless of the amounts, should be completely transparent and reported to the IRS. This would allow Congressional officials to interact with the constituents while in their districts, instead of lobbyist and special interest groups. Ideally, politicians should only be allowed to use personal funds or public Federal Campaign Funds, but we will never see this happen in our lifetime. This will avoid enormous donations from individuals, activist organizations, or corporations, which are the cancer of the system. Furthermore, by utilizing public funds, this will avoid any misunderstanding or problems with transparencies of campaign support funds. Maybe it is time for the American people to organize and demand these changes in our political system and return to the basic principles of our founding fathers.

It seems that politicians tend to forget that they are the representatives of their constituents or population that elected them into office. Instead of acting like our representatives in the House of Representatives and the Senate, they ignore the needs of the people in their districts. They are supposed to introduce legislation that satisfies the needs of their constituents, but instead what they concentrate on is supporting the interest of those individuals that provide financial support for their campaigns. True legislation in support of their constituents is non-existent, and what they introduce is self-interest or that of their political parties' agenda. They have the tendency to assume the responsibility of "thinking" for us, as if we were a population composed of morons or had "stupid" tattooed on our foreheads, by insulting our degree of intelligence. If you contact them through their congressional office telephone lines or the internet, they have a young staffer answering your concerns or some standard congressional letterhead with a "nonsense standard response" signed by an "iron hand." Even a child can see and understand that this is to appease the constituents or just to respond in order to stop people from bothering them. Nowadays the new way to stop those constituents that show concern about an issue is by having the lines disconnected, busy, or answering machines full. If you use the internet to send electronic correspondence, the mailbox is full. I wonder if it will be better to elect the staffers into office, because they are more "in tune" with what is going on with the constituency, than of the actual elected official.

It seems that all elected officials during the swearing in ceremony, sign a contract to vote and support their political party. They introduce bills and vote down party lines, instead of what is good for the nation or their constituents. This applies to both major political parties, because if you put a politician of each party in a brown bag and shake it, you cannot tell one from the other when they fall out. This is especially true when they are in the majority because they try to introduce all their pet projects as quickly as possible. They legislate at the speed of lightning, for fear of losing support, being voted out, or losing the majority in Congress. The saddest part of this practice is that most of the legislation introduced by either the Speaker of the House of Representatives or Majority Leader of the Senate is not read in order to make an intelligent decision on the vote. They have no shame, because they tell you outright that they have not read the legislation. Amazingly, most are lawyers and do not understand the language as it is written. They use the excuse that it cannot be in a simple language, because it can be challenged in court. Again, we should elect their staffers or the person who speed-reads all the legislation, because these are the people that really know what is going on in Congress. All legislation is crafted and dealt with in committees and the only thing that our elected officials do is to add pet or pork projects, with the approval of the leader. It seems that they take turns in whose pork or pet project is going to be inserted in the legislation to pass to the President for signature. They do not care how they spend our tax money or how they waste it. Legislation that they don't want the people to know about or express resentment or disapproval, they pass even more quickly or it's inserted in major legislation at the last minute, prior to the final vote. As most of the elected officials are lawyers, legislation is purposely crafted in a language that no one can read or understand, even when it is posted on the internet for everyone to see. All legislation should be written in plain language that all Americans could read and understand, ideally with ample time for input to their representative. On the contrary, they do not, but then have the gall to stand in front of all Americans on national television and make statements to the effect that "the American people don't care about a little pork." When it comes to millions and millions of dollars in pet or pork projects, you can bet your last penny that we care about how our tax money is wasted. I hope that most Americans care too. What we have to do is to take notes and remember all these practices, when it comes election time. All these officials that think they are at a level above the American people in intelligence, will be in for a big surprise.

It seems the golden rule for a politician, when he or she decides to run for office, to find all of those individuals who are financially independent to finance or support their campaigns. Now I understand the mission of political exploratory committees, which does nothing more than to gather as many multi-millionaires, media people and corporations to finance the campaigns. Common sense tells me, that you do not invest millions of dollars just because the candidate is nice looking, a person with a good heart, great personality, or love of their country. This support comes with a lot of strings attached and is usually payback on a large scale with government contracts, pet projects, or legislation in favor of any given agenda.

Similarly, political candidates have the tendency to gather as many ex-politicians as possible, to teach them "the ropes," and to ensure their political position in any place in the government. This applies to both parties because neither one is different or free of guilt. They rehash these old politicians and name them as advisors, in cabinet positions of the White House, in Congress, any place possible within the government. Most of these rehashed politicians have more skeletons in their closet than a haunted house on Halloween. They are usually from previous administrations or a majority in Congress when any given party is in control. The worst thing about this practice is, these rehashed career politicians answer to no one, because they are not elected nor are they confirmed by Congress and they have the freedom to do whatever they want. They seldom have any new ideas and provide no change to the business as usual in Washington. The elected official turns a blind eye, because usually they are key personnel in their re-election process and are needed by the person in office. Our government in Washington is like a "garage sale," buying and selling off old "geezers" with no real solutions to the problems of the nation. The comedy is the new name for these individuals, the "Czars" who in some cases have no knowledge of what they are doing or the people they are suppose to oversee for government malpractices. It is like hoodlums serving as jurors for another hoodlum who is being prosecuted, in the end, you know the result. The reason for this conclusion is that most Czars were in charge of previous agencies or institutions, which were failures, so now they are in charge of a program by the current administration.

I will highlight some of the pet peeves that I have with our deteriorating form of government in the last three decades, which I will pinch some nerves, because the truth hurts and no one likes to hear it. These problems affect all Americans and I am sure that they are worth reminding the people, so that people can take notes for the next time they go to the polls. I am sure this affects you, your family, and your community as a whole.

Although most of the present elected officials are attorneys and they have a great knowledge of the laws and the United States Constitution, it seems that they have the tendency to insult the degree of intelligence of all Americans. They think that they rule the world and are above the law of the land. Some of these attorneys, as representative of the people, are suppose to enforce and defend the laws, but become the worst offenders in this nation and are not held accountable for this practice. Regardless of his or her years of higher education to receive his or her law degree, we do not need anyone to think for us. They usually flash their degrees from these four more famous schools in the nation, but if we are old enough to cast a vote and elect them, we are intelligent and old enough to think for ourselves. We do not need anyone to think for us, but to fight for our interest as our representatives in Congress. No wonder some people in the media think that this is a nation of "dummies." Maybe we are, for electing and re-electing these individuals, sending them to Washington as our representatives repeatedly. It is time to wake up and start making the proper demands from our elected officials. If we get a negative response, get rid of them. All elected officials are supposed to be held to the highest ethical standards. In the last three decades, politicians of both parties, leave a whole lot to be desired. It seems that almost every six months, they surprise us with a new scandal. Both parties have ethical investigative committees, but it seems that the only thing they investigate is the other party. They do it to make national news, with the support of their media goons, to gain political points. When I hear this in the news, it irks me, but reminds me of what my grandfather use to tell me. The Chinese mantra states, "You must have respect for yourself, you must have respect for all others and you must be responsible for all your actions." This is something that is non-existent in Washington, among our politicians or their advisors. Maybe we will be lucky enough in our lifetime, to see the bar raised, and our system will be better for all the American people.

Every time there is a change of power in government, regardless if it is Congress, or the White House, they never take responsibility for the position or office for which they have been elected. In real life, in any organization, you are responsible for all duties the date you are sworn in or assume that position. Politicians are the only ones that are not and use the excuse that they inherited the problems. The only time they assume responsibility, is when things are going well. If they run for elected office, it is because they are qualified. They should take responsibility the first day they take over the position and whatever they inherit, that includes the good, bad, or ugly, the first day they are sworn in. They think they are smarter than we are, but after campaigning for over a year and listening to the news, they should know what they are getting into. When you keep hearing, with support of the media, that you inherited problems and you do not have a solution, then you should resign your position because you are not qualified. Go and practice law in the private sector. If you replace someone in Washington D.C., it is because the American people consider the previous person to be incompetent, not doing a good job and are giving someone else the opportunity to change things that are not going well. The politician should use his or her initiative to take corrective action, instead of finding excuses to justify the lack of qualifications. The American people are so desperate for solutions to the problems of the nation and change of the business as usual in Washington, that if a cartoon character with the right financial support would run for office, they would vote for him. Proof of this lately, is that we are sending comedians, activists or whatever to Washington in the hope of a real change, even if they do not have a clue about the office.

According to Webster's dictionary, a leader is a well-rounded individual with a commanding authority to be the head of a body or group. My understanding of a well-rounded person is someone with experience in all facets or situations in life, in either the private sector or government. A person exposed to a myriad of experiences and jobs at different levels; or ethnic groups, not only during elections; has traveled and dealt with other leaders and can relate to people of different levels. A well-rounded person with common sense is able to make decisions to complicated problems independently, which will satisfy the needs of the majority. A person with just plain seniority or occupying space in the same position for years is not a well-rounded individual, especially when the only job they have ever held in their life is in politics or with the government. A person that is not independent enough, or lacks the backbone to vote on issues regardless of party lines, is not well rounded. To me that is a person who, has been in the right place at the right time, is financially independent or has the financial support from a group of individuals to initiate a career as a politician. When politicians throw the term "leadership" around in Washington D.C. describing a person or a group of individuals, it reminds me of a pack of wolves. The one that barks or growls the loudest or is the most devious, is the one elected as the leader of the pack. This does not mean that it is the most experienced or smartest of the pack. The rest of the pack just follows; "smelling and kissing butt" until the chosen one dies or is unable to "lead," then it is their turn to become the leader of the pack. Every time they mention the name of a politician with the title of leader, or one that has leadership, it encourages me to research their backgrounds to match the title with their intelligence, qualifications, or experiences. A trial lawyer only has experience in court with plea-bargaining for their criminals. Although they know the law and they can get away with a whole lot, this does not mean they necessarily possess leadership traits. This only qualifies them to make "shady" deals and enhance their careers. A community activist, besides protesting and "making waves," does not fall in my category of well-rounded individual, but more in the category of growling the loudest. A Wall Street broker is not necessarily, what I call well rounded; it is more in the category of a wheeler and dealer. A comedian, a good example that anything can happen in this country, is real proof that this is the land of opportunities. With all do respect, a homemaker is better rounded than those whose first job is in politics. She is better qualified because she deals with savings and pay as you go, manages, and sticks to the home budget and within those parameters, can still meet the needs of the majority of the household. A person 'born into money" just has money, notoriety and a name which opens doors and nothing else. Usually this group falls in the category of "air heads with an attitude." Career civil service employees, who are political appointees, do not fall into the well-rounded category either, usually this group falls in the "butt kissing" group. Although there are a very few, that are well rounded and could fall in this category of leaders, these have the tendency to be modest and behind the scenes, they are not placed in the so-called "political leadership" positions. Sometimes they lose their traits, out of frustration, and turn into followers and join the majority of losers. It's amazing how the great majority of politicians think the majority of Americans are impressed when they stand in front of a national television camera and start throwing these titles and phrases like confetti, such as "the great leadership of Jane or Joe Blow head of the candy store committee" or "under the leadership of Jane or Joe Blow," when introducing questionable legislation. It is like watching a comedy show. What is sad is that they have their entourage of staffers and "journalists," who eat this up, ready to put the remarks of these news conferences on the front page of a newspaper or as "breaking news" on television. What is worse is that they think, or are convinced, that most of the American people believe all this horse manure. America please read, think, and analyze! All I am saying is, these are what we have in Washington, in charge of what is suppose to be the most powerful nation in the world.

I always believe that when someone is going to make a decision that affects the lives and future of thousands of men and women, they should have the necessary experience in the field for which they are making the decision. I do not like to use percentages, because I am not a statistician, but I know for sure that at least an eighty percent of the people in Congress have never served in the military. So logically, by not having military experience, how can they make those sensitive decisions that affect so many families and the lives of military personnel alike. Military expertise and tactics, no matter how smart you are, cannot be learned or be acquired through college or reading a book; but through experience in the "trenches." I am a firm believer that if you did not wear my boots, or invest blood, sweat and tears, you have not earned the right to tell me what to do. Some of these activist groups, media personnel, and even politicians cannot point on a map the location where the military is involved in any type of conflict. This is the reason it is hard for me to understand how a so-called, "political leader" makes an intelligent decision when it comes to national defense, without the necessary military experience or expertise. Furthermore, those appointed career politicians, or so-called advisors who make these decisions, are like the blind leading the blind. They should be grateful that there are still some senior military personnel available to guide them, but sometimes the sound, intelligent advice from these personnel is ignored because it does not agree with their agenda. What is extremely sad is that politicians make decisions under pressure from a small population of ungrateful citizens, who tend to forget that if not for the sacrifice that these men and women have given to the nation, they have the freedom and opportunity to express their ignorance, would not exist. You must remember that most politicians have no integrity and listen to or comply with the wishes of these groups, because it equals votes and re-election. Based on the decisions of politicians, this attitude towards the military has spread all around the nation and there are some specific states that even ban the presence of military personnel in certain locations. What is hilarious is that when there is a natural disaster or any type of emergency or need of protection, the first people these politicians and states call for assistance, are the military. As an individual, that has dedicated most of my adult life serving and defending this nation, it turns my stomach when I hear these individual's statements and other protests towards the military. I guess the only thing they appreciate from the military is Memorial Day, because they do not honor those who sacrificed their lives for the nation, but it gives them a holiday to barbecue and drink beer. The other misconception that the general population has is the erroneous opinion that most people in the military are a bunch of dummies that only joined the military because of a lack of education, training, or opportunities to make it in the "elite" civilian life. There are dedicated military families who have educated sons and daughters that serve in the military, out of love of country and tradition. Something that is presently lacking in this nation. Nevertheless, every society needs a variety of all things, just as much as you need a little of dumb, dumber and stupid to complete our nation. In fact, the worse decision made by politicians was to abolish the military draft. A law that every nation around the world has to instill values, appreciation for your freedom, and pride and love of country. The draft provided discipline, respect, and training to most of the male population, which is something that is non-existent nowadays in this nation. Something is desperately needed to teach our young population values combined with respect and discipline, in its absence. This is the reason why the majority of the young people in this nation are out of control, with no pride of country and they think they deserve everything. We should be grateful and kiss the ground where we stand, because there are still some men and women that with their service have not forgotten and see the world and appreciate what they have. When I listen to politicians and those that have no sense of respect for this nation and express their stupidity, I pray and repeat with a whole lot of respect the phrase "God Bless America." Politicians do not completely understand that in an attempt to "protect" their sons and daughters, they have caused greater harm to the nation by eliminating the military draft.

This is the point where I do not only pinch some nerves, but also turn some faces like a rainbow, because of anger or hatred. Politicians of both parties, have the tendency to appease part of the population to "avoid discrimination, expand opportunities and represent the less fortunate" by passing some laws that, in my opinion, have caused the opposite of the original goal. I do not agree with the fact that millions of our tax dollars go to support certain activist organizations because the tax codes apply to all Americans and should benefit all citizens. As most politicians are lawyers, they support some activist organizations that, with the excuse that they defend the less fortunate, have become the watchdogs of issues that do not agree with their views. I have made a pledge not to name organizations or individuals, consequently I will not start now, but the majority of the American people understand who and what I am referring. I do give them credit because these individuals are extremely astute and have a team of researchers that find a way to "turn the wheels" to their advantage. You also have to give them credit because they are so persistent, that they do not stop until they get what they are looking for. I personally do not have anything against any of these activist organizations as long as they are not functioning on my "dime." As a taxpayer, I also have the right to be against this practice by politicians, because to me they are wasting my tax dollars. If politicians want support from these organizations, the expenses should be provided from their own personal funds or their campaign money, if legal, or from the tooth fairy. Taxpayer's monies should be for the benefit of the entire population and not for the few. I continue to repeat that, if we are going to "level the playing field," let it be level for every American. It is sad but researching these organizations, I found that a few take advantage of the great majority and abuse their ignorance and lack of education to manipulate them, by providing political support for some politicians in exchange for federal funding to the "heads" of these activities. In turn, they receive millions of dollars from Congress for this political activism to elect them into office. Again, I have been known to tell it as I see it, and cannot stop now. I guess that to receive the benefits of social government programs, you must pay a price. What is a shame is that they are encouraged by some of their own minority "leaders," in the name of equal rights and civil liberties, to allow this to happen. You have to give them credit because they are extremely intelligent and have been able to diversify their ideology, through different organizations with the same purpose. Politicians give these individuals the blind eye because they satisfy their needs of being elected to office. They are so astute that they have spread like the "swine flu" all over the nation and with the help of high elected officials and multi-millionaires that want to control the nation, they are almost unstoppable. Another sad fact is, minorities have not figured out their purpose, nor have they gained or advanced a step towards what they were promised. Education remains the same, housing remains the same and job opportunities have not changed. Wealth distribution will never happen in this nation because when pressured, the rich will "take their money and run" and the poor will remain poor. Expansion of the government will collapse without the tax revenue and the vicious cycle will start again. Meanwhile, the poor are the ones most affected, the federal government will not do a thing for the poor, and they will continue in their same status. The answer is to educate you, be prepared, and work hard to have a better life. Nothing in this world is free and those that promise you wealth and a better status of living are getting rich with your efforts and will "take your money and run." Open your eyes and take control of your life and that of your loved ones because promises are only promises and nothing will fall from the sky soon. If you see or find a poor politician or one that cares about you let me know. They start wealthy and finish multi-millionaires and their only interest in you, is your vote. That is the reason why they fight with all their might to be elected and re-elected into office, no matter what the cost.

The judicial system is another branch of government that we need to keep a close eye on, to ensure that the rule of law is applied with blind eyes and in an equal manner to every American. This is another branch of government that needs drastic changes as the Supreme Court Justices should be appointed and confirmed for a period no longer than ten years, instead of a lifetime appointment. This will ensure that all political bias is eliminated in the system and justice is applied equally to all Americans. Our whole system has to be brought under control, as there is no equality in the application of punishments and penalties across the whole United States. Justice should be blind and free of politics. Our political views should be taken out of the judicial system. Judges should be appointed on experience and merits, not on political views, ideology, or quotas to appease the population. Sometimes it gives the impression that your punishment is dependent on your financial status, political connections, or the influence that your defense attorney has with the court. Prosecutors have a lot to do with this problem because of the plea-bargaining they do with defense attorneys and judges. It seems that if you are a celebrity or a white-collar professional, the laws and the penalties are different from those of blue-collar workers, minorities, or people of less influence. The best comedy show is when our politicians go on prime time television to nominate and confirm judges to the United States Supreme Court or Appellate Courts. Our politicians in the majority, this applies to both parties, go through a televised show of interrogation, questions and answers to find out if a political nominee to the court is qualified to serve. Regardless of their qualifications, the majority will nominate and confirm the person that the President selects or nominates anyway. It is like a "make believe" game to show the American people that the nominee was scrutinized by Congress to ascertain their qualifications. When I see these games politicians play, I am convinced that they think the American people are stupid. Usually no matter what goes on, there will be a certain number of judges with a tendency to rule with an ideology in favor of one party or the other, dependent upon which party is in the White House or has the majority in Congress. The comical part is that if a judge wants or has the intention to retire from the bench, they will wait until the right President is in power in order to be replaced by the a judge of the same political ideology. It is cynical but "Lady Justice" plays "peek-a-boo" and looks the way convenient to the party in power. Judges that do not apply the applicable laws of the land should be disbarred after a written warning. Since the judicial system is so corrupt and prostituted, the law is applied in accordance to the principles and ideology of the political party in power. In order to simplify the process, judges should be required to retire when their political party is in power. They should lay down the requirements that the political party wants. For instance, if the nominee is from the left, he or she should have empathy, be of a minority group, or have great experience or background with the poor to apply the law. If the nominee is from the right, the laws should be applied with conservative principles. The reason that I suggest this methods of nominating and confirming these judges is to avoid the charade that the Senate goes through for weeks, insulting the level of intelligence of the American people. They do not comply with the principles that our founding fathers envisioned, so stopped the charade. The whole process is like a Broadway show because you do not expect that the majority is going to ask tough questions, or that the nominee is going to be honest in answering the questions so as not to jeopardize their confirmation. They hide their bias well and justify any previous mistake with a fairytale story in order to reach their goal. I cannot stop being sarcastic because the roles these politicians play deserve an academy award because they even cry, in the name of the American people. This will eliminate this waste of time and allow them to deal with issues that are of more interest to all citizens, rather than this farce. Furthermore, this should also apply to the appointment of cabinet positions, the same rules. It should be like appointing a Czar that does not need congressional approval. The only one they answer to is the President. Most of them have no qualifications to do the job. The Supreme Court also needs to have a close eye kept on them, with term limits needed in order to ensure swift rulings. Every administration, from every political party, has come with a brilliant idea of naming the so-called Czar to serve as watchdog and regulate the people's interest. These Czars are just political favors as they do not know what they're supposed to do, answer to no one and are part of the "gang" that they're suppose to foresee or regulate and basically end up doing nothing. This practice should end with the next administration or elected President. Although it has been going on forever, it will be extremely difficult to bring an end to, or "unfair" to terminate, with the present administration. We should demand our elected officials to introduce legislation to curtail the size of government with these appointed political favors. Also, require that all political appointees, that regulate or dictate policies in the government, be investigated or at least qualified for the position and be confirmed by Congress prior to being appointed. Now they have too much power and answer to no one about their decisions that affect the whole nation.

Punishment for non law-abiding citizens should be like a menu in a restaurant. The degree of the crime should equal the amount of years or months in prison with no plea bargaining, house arrests or parole for any reason. Those that find religion in prison, continue to pray that they do not commit a crime again, should not be able to use this as a reason for parole. You should serve the full sentence of your punishment, with no exceptions; this will certainly be a deterrent for those who commit crimes. Recurrent offenders should be punished with higher penalties, and juveniles that commit major crimes should be tried as adults. Our present system has a rotating door, where offenders come in and out, because of the leniency of the courts and prison system. I have the highest respect for life and do not believe in capital punishment because no one has the right to take anyone else's life. I do not believe that a criminal should be a burden to society for the rest of his or her life, either. Prisons should be built in an area that allows the prisoners to be self sufficient, allowing them to grow their own food and no special privileges that will be a burden to the law-abiding citizens. I might sound a little cynical but if the government builds a major prison complex on Johnston Island, with no television, internet, or telephones and allow them to grow their own food, this would be a solution to our problem. You will save millions in building more prisons, government contracts to run the prison, prison guards, electricity, all the amenities given in prison and food with no risks of prison breaks. The activist groups, lawyers, and human rights people will have a field day with all types of complaints about human rights violations, but the government should take a stand and consider the rights of those that the crime has been committed upon, because they have rights too. If you are found guilty and go to prison, it is to comply with a prison sentence, not to go to a country club. The current prison facilities will be utilized for minor crimes. Because we have so many prisons, all others can be converted into educational or vocational institutions and camps for our youth. All we have to provide to those who break the law is a fair trial by their peers with appropriate representation. Regardless of the ethnicity of the criminals, financial status, or age of the individual, this should apply to everyone who breaks the law, end of story. I will guarantee that the crime rate will diminish in less than three years, with no recurrent offenders or those that escape prison endangering the rest of the population. For those attorneys and people in Washington who know it all, this is your homework, to find the location of Johnston Island on a map.

There are only few names that I use in this book with the utmost respect and one of them is that of Dr. Martin Luther King Jr. A man of respect, integrity and admired by many who fought for a just cause, but it is a shame that he could not see his dream come true. If he would have been alive today, he could have seen his dream come true with the 2008 Presidential election. He would have seen that his fight for equal rights and civil liberties was not in vain. The only problem is that many civil rights leaders, in my opinion, are using his name in vain and abusing his cause. The late John F. Kennedy and his brother Robert Kennedy initiated the movement towards approval of the Civil Rights Act and ended discrimination and segregation in this country. President Lyndon B. Johnson signed the Civil Rights Act in 1964, which provided equal rights for all citizens of this nation. My question is that if the Civil Rights Act was approved and signed forty-five years ago, until when are we going to abuse Affirmation Action. It is justifiable that anyone who's over the age of forty-five, needed the Affirmative Action because of the injustices committed in the nation due to lack of civil liberties, equal opportunities and discrimination. They needed this special law to give them the opportunities that they were deprived of prior to the Civil Rights Act. Anyone who is younger than forty-five years of age, in my opinion, has no excuse not to take advantage of the present opportunities and should compete under their own merits in education and job opportunities. I do not understand why my children and those of the great majority of Americans, have to continue to pay for the injustices and for something that they were not part of. Until when should children and adults alike, of the great majority of the population be in debt or pay for injustices that happened before they were born? Is this going to be a never-ending debt to minorities and people of color and all their future generations? It is time to turn the page, move forward, and look ahead for better things earned by our own merits. As I mentioned before, this should be part of our education in history, to ensure that it never happens again. To correct part of the problems, we should start with education, which starts at home with proper guidance and good study habits. It also starts with parents being part of the educational process of their children to ensure independence from the federal government, instead of promoting dependency from social programs. We should provide the opportunity to all those who want to study and will take advantage of the public education, as provided by the federal government like everyone else has done in this nation. Those who want to pursue higher education should commit themselves to study in order to compete like everybody else, by preparing themselves and studying for all necessary entrance examinations and requirements. There should not be any double standards for different ethnic groups or quotas to appease any minority. Educational assistance should also be on a competitive basis for every young man or woman who applies for it and qualifies on scholastic merits. This applies also to job opportunities. Special consideration should not be given to any minority. The majority of children in this nation, mine included, have received a public education and have done fine. The excuse that certain minorities are under privileged and they are not able to receive a good education is old, worn out and bogus. Schools nowadays are integrated, where there are students of all ethnic groups, and they all receive the same educational programs. Some excel and others not. The schools and educational programs are not the problems, although it is true that some schools have unqualified teachers, but the same curriculum applies to all ethnic groups. Part of the problem is that parents should demand educational excellence from their children and they refuse to do so. Again, if Affirmative Action applies to some, it should apply to all. Although there is no such thing as reverse discrimination, the color of your skin or lack thereof, should not be a qualifier for education or job opportunities. Today we have minorities as outstanding scholars, successful professionals in all fields and heads of major corporations who had the same inner-city background, but have taken advantage of all opportunities of this great nation and have excelled. I admire the success of these few that have taken the responsibility and worked hard to get ahead. I refuse to accept that the failure of the majority is because they are complacent and accept mediocrity, or due to do dependency on the federal government and their social programs with no end at sight. They refused to be another statistic and with the help of devoted parents, they work hard to climb and reach the pyramid of success. If these few have been able to get ahead with no special favors, then what are the excuses from the others that are not successful in accomplishing these goals? We should stop encouraging or promoting the idea of becoming professional sports stars, becoming rap singers or Hollywood stars, because these careers do not last long. A great number of politicians and civil rights leaders ignore the accomplishments of these individuals in order to continue to take advantage of this legislation. It seems that a great number of civil rights leaders do not want minorities to get ahead on their merits, because they won't have the excuse of discrimination and energize the minority population. They always cry and throw the words racist or racism around, because that is how they keep "the movement" alive and the federal government will bend backwards to appease their demands and continue federal funding for whatever endeavor they get involved in or any tax exemption. Additionally, without "the movement" and federal funding, these civil rights leaders will be like everyone else and have to find a real nine to five job and will be out of the news media, crying foul. Some civil right leaders and activist groups are all around the nation with a magnifying glass in order to find any type of incident, to make the news and justify "their existence" to the federal government and politicians. They will throw the words racist or racism as fast as lightning and label anyone as a racist for their advantage. The danger is that they will destroy innocent lives, without caring about the results. I just hope, for the best interest of the nation, that they would apologize publicly when they are wrong as quickly as when they accuse someone who is innocent. In order for this nation to move ahead and to turn the page, people will have to, hopefully, start with a clean slate because enough is enough. We cannot continue with this inequity because it produces anger, discontentment, and real racism, if we do not stop.

I had purposely ignored discussing all the "lightning legislation" process that we are experiencing by the Washington D.C. gang, of both political parties. Presently, the majority in Congress is trying to shove down the throat of the American people a myriad of legislations that are of the utmost importance to all citizens without considering the disservice they are doing to all taxpayers. The reason is because the previous majority of a different party did the same thing in the "name of fiscal responsibility" and this party is doing it in the "name of change." These politicians have driven us into the largest debt this nation has ever experienced, which our children and grandchildren will have to pay. Now they have come up with these brilliant ideas about social medicine and save the environment or global warming, and Cap and Trade, which will increase the taxes of hard working American because what they impose on corporations is passed to the consumers. I am using these legislations as an example, but the specific legislations are immaterial, what is important is the process in which they pass the legislation. In my opinion, they insult our intelligence and you should be aware and demand an explanation of any "lightning legislation" from your elected official. The "justifiable excuse," is that the minority in Congress has forgotten that the present majority inherited a deficit from the other party's previous administration. Consequently, they can continue to pull one over on us. The other justifiable argument is that their party's administration, two decades ago, left a surplus but they forget that this was due to high taxes. These are all excuses to pass legislation of their pet and pork projects before they are voted out of power as the majority. The pointing of guilty fingers continues. Sorry to use this expression, but if they think the rich Americans will continue to sponsor all these social programs with higher taxes, they might have mental retardation. If you can single out any poor man or woman in elected office, you win the Washington Memorial. What they are pushing is, for people to quit being successful, because it is not worth working hard for the government to take the fruits of your labor and give it to those who do not want to work. Our system is designed to take a chance, being successful and enjoy the fruits of your success. Robin Hood died in the forest in Europe a very long time ago. Additionally, they will not invest or expand their businesses, but rather, outsource their businesses to other countries or lay-off employees and in the end; the ones who suffer are the American people. The principles of this nation are to make the right choices, work hard, and be successful. If the government is going to penalize you for making the right choices, then let us all be on welfare and food stamps, enjoy all the social programs, and be dependent on the federal government. Apparently, this is what politicians want in order to control our lives. Additionally, if the politicians want to take control of all our financial institutions, private industries and control our freedom, let us go all the way and become like our neighbors Cuba and Venezuela, which are the closest on the American Continent, as examples. At the rate we are going, it seems that this is the end goal of the "ruling party" – doesn't this sound familiar? You make your own decision after you analyze what is happening. I do not want to sound political, but after all that I have invested in this nation, it irks me to see how we are allowing a few, maybe a thousand men and women in Washington D.C. to control millions of us.

Something that I am reluctant to discuss is the United States foreign policy. The reason is, as I previously stated, I have dedicated most of my adult life serving and defending this nation. I am such a fool that, if I had to do it again, I would be the first in line. Politicians, the media, and the general population should count their blessings because of the dedication of brilliant young men and women that are willing to make the ultimate sacrifice for this nation, in the name of love of country. Although I am not a self-proclaimed strategist like those that appear in the media, but just an average American, I will make a recount of my experiences during the opportunity to travel around the world while defending this nation. This is something that a great number of "self proclaimed experts or politicians" do not have. Not every one around the world, like us, use good will and soft hearts. If the dollar had full value and was worth more than their currency, they would scream "Yankee go home and leave your dollar," but now they only say "Yankee go home." Most of the young generation in many countries, hate us with a passion and do not hide it. Only the older generation, especially in Europe, remembers what we did for them in World War II and are still grateful and appreciative of our sacrifices. It is completely different in East and Southwest Asia where there is some resentment against the United States. I am confused that politicians with all their education as lawyers have not studied history. How can you give in to dictators that hate the American capitalistic system and standards of living? With all the blood that many young men and women have sacrificed, they want to have one-on-one talks with these people and appease their demands. It is hard to understand why the words "terrorist and terrorism" have been taken out of our vocabulary, after the attacks on this nation. Contrary to the summits, conferences and all the Gs around the world, many nations only call upon the United States when they are in need of our defense or financial needs. Assistance is a two way street and we should require other nations to reciprocate, when we are in need of any type of assistance. After all, we have taken the burden of defending freedom and democracy around the world, putting the burden on our military. The American people are always present to assist in any type of emergency or catastrophe and be there for the world with defense, medical aide, and funds to assist all nations. Sorry, but let me open some eyes of the general population and politicians alike; we are no longer considered or treated as the number one super power of the world. If we were still on top, a great number of nations would not be thumbing their noses at us or ignoring our threats of sanctions for their misbehavior. If you analyze the situation with nations in East and Southwest Asia, not even the United Nations, takes us seriously even though we fund most of their operations. Other nations ignore our requests for assistance in applying sanctions to nations that thumb their noses because they want to see us go under. The same applies on our own continent. Merely look at our neighbors in Central and South America and the Caribbean, where even "third world" nations thumb their noses. This has been going on for at least the past three decades with whichever Secretary of State, male or female, with or without experience that the past administrations have nominated for the position. Sorry to tell you the truth but they all failed, with or without great deals to appease the needs of the country they have dealt with and are thumbing their noses. America, we should wake up and stop buying friends and allies around the world because it is not working. Just look at the support that we have received with Iraq and Afghanistan, "the illegal war" and the "right war" as they are called by politicians and the media. It has been minimal and in support capacity, not fighting warriors. It is worth mentioning that because Afghanistan is this administration and party's war, there is no count of lost soldier's lives, the cost or funding has not been highlighted by the party or the media. They purposely forget that when you are sworn in for service, you fight and wear the uniform in the name of the United States, and not a political party to the left or the right. The present policy guidelines of talking, shaking hands and providing assistance to all nations is not working and will not work because we live in a world of self-preservation and survival, where everyone is out for themselves. We have to change our policy because the present ones are not working and all we are doing is wasting taxpayer's monies that can be better utilized here at home now that our nation's economy is in shambles. We are lying to the American people and ourselves; instead, we should take a step back and regroup to develop a better foreign policy that will work. As a matter of a little lesson in history, when the Soviet Union got involved in the war in Afghanistan, they fought for six or seven years and the result was that they could not do it by themselves. The Afghanistan war abolished their form of government and they finished as a Russia with no money, a destroyed military and had to retreat without winning the war. This should be a lesson learned by our inexperienced politicians in Washington that have taken this war to prove that the previous administration was wrong by fighting the war against terrorism in the wrong theater. Another thing that my father used to tell me was, "When people get excited, they cannot think straight and always make the wrong decisions." Let history teach us the lesson we need, before we make our military sacrifice so many lives for a lost cause. Furthermore, if we are going to continue going into Afghanistan, we should look at this as a coalition of countries, and not just the United States going alone. Politicians should listen to those in the military with experience, prior to sending our military into harm's way. If they are not committed to win any conflict, they should restrain from sending young men and women. We should stop using "political strategy" when making decisions that affect so many lives in this nation. To appease political support, by sacrificing lives and the security of the nation is completely wrong. Listening to the so-called experts and advisors, in the administration and the media, is frightening because of the lack of expertise. Their political agenda will not allow them to see past their noses and they have no viable solution to the problems, only rhetoric to appease political supporters. They ignore the military brass with experience, only, to listen to those with protesting experiences.

I will take advantage and "piggyback" on our foreign policy because there is something that has had me perplexed for years. Again, I will pinch some nerves, but somebody has to bring it out. In simple American terms, if you put your cookies in a cookie jar and someone else does not, they have no right to take any cookies. What I am trying to say is that after researching the statutes of Puerto Rico and Guam, I see some unfairness to their position. As a Commonwealth, they have their own flags, do not pay federal income tax, have representation in Congress, albeit without a vote, and enjoy all the rights of American citizenship. What is confusing about the whole situation is that although they do not pay federal taxes, they enjoy the fruits of social programs and the assistance that comes with all these benefits. The only ones that are required to pay federal taxes are those that work for the federal government, but as complicated as the system is, they get a return of these taxes through their commonwealth system. Corporations and businesses that are established in Puerto Rico and Guam are not required to pay federal taxes either. What is annoying is that with their representation in Washington, they are allowed to lobby in Congress for their commonwealth. Another annoying fact is that they very proudly display their own flags and compete in world events as independent nations. My question is then, why can't they have as referendum or plebiscite and decide once and for all, if they want to be a part of the Union as a state or if they want to be independent. If they decide, they want independence, then let them go, without the benefits. Those that want to be independent can no longer can enjoy the privileges of citizenship, unless the choice is to be American citizens. If they will continue to enjoy the privileges of social programs, they should be required to pay federal taxes. It is no different from paying federal and state taxes, like everyone else. This will "level the playing field" for everyone and alleviate the burden to the majority of American citizens paying taxes to defray the cost of their social programs. It is important to highlight the fact that many citizens from these two commonwealths have contributed their service to the military. Their personal contribution is of such importance that some have paid the ultimate sacrifice, which is something that many in the mainland have not done. They have shown more love of country, which is lacking today in many of the American people. This is something that you should bring to the attention of your elected officials when they come soliciting your precious vote. Furthermore, I do not believe in the use of "hyphen American." The only ones that, in my opinion can do hyphen American are those who are not natural-born or have not taken their citizenship. When you have taken the oath, you are sworn to obey the Constitution and at the end, it says 'Welcome

American citizen,' not hyphen. It is good to honor your roots and never forget where you came from, but if you are native born or become a citizen, you should be proud to be an American.

As you can see, the government has the greatest impact on your lives and the achievement of the American Dream for you, your children, and all future generations. You should ensure that you demand term limits from your elected officials to avoid that they become career politicians, dead wood, waste your tax monies, and provide no representation for your district in Washington D.C. As they will not change the system because is not in their best interest, kick them out of office by not re-electing them, unless they are doing their job and are worth keeping in Washington. No longer than three terms, however, because that is when corruption kicks in. You have the most powerful weapon, with your vote, to stop all the corruption and abuse in Washington. With all the over spending in "pork and pet projects" that doesn't benefit you or your immediate family, the take over of our industries and job producing entities and total control of our assets by the government, we should put a stop to this practice. Do not allow politicians to make you dependent on the federal government and control your lives, on the contrary, take charge of your lives and future. Prepare yourself and your children to be successful and reach the top. I do not advocate violence and I am completely against it. If you have the ability to though, organize leagues, charity drives or participate in "tea parties" and stand up for your rights. Again, utilize the best weapon you have, which is your vote to fight back against corruption and end all the government's legislations that do not do anything for you or your family. Do not re-elect politicians that ignore your needs or those of your community or state. You should vote with your brain and not your heart, sympathy or any party line. Be independent from those politicians that only come to see you during elections. Please do not prostitute your vote for a library, monument, road, or a bridge to nowhere, think, and make the right decision when you cast your vote. You as a community or an organized group can peacefully make a difference, if you care and want the best for this nation and that of future generations. Protest against the federal assistance to financial organizations, Wall Street, special interest organizations, activist organizations, political support, unions, and industries that will go bankrupt with or without the federal assistance. At the pace that politicians are spending and the debt incurred, they will take this nation to the point of no return and soon we will be a third world country. If you are afraid that there is going to be a major terrorist attack, have peace of mind and don't be afraid because those who hate our system of government and our standard of living are just watching as our politicians are leading us down the path of self destruction. They should have a bellyache from so much laughing in their caves in the mountains of Afghanistan or Pakistan, or wherever they are in Southwest Asia. The only ones that are caught are those that are looking for attention and are minor cells of real terrorist groups. You are the only ones that can make a change and not a politician in Washington with false promises that worsens everything in our nation. The answer is in your hands and on your shoulders. Consequently use your brain and stick to your convictions when making your decisions, because contrary to what some people want you to believe, you are intelligent, levelheaded and are capable to make excellent choices, which will make the difference. Do not make the wrong choices out of frustration and then regret it for the next two or four years. The change that politicians offer you is only during the campaign period and ends when they get to Washington. They suffer amnesia and forget what change they promised. The only change they have offered so far is from one political party to another. Remember that if you put two politicians from different parties in a brown bag and shake it, all you get is more of the same. This is a great nation, but we should return to what our founding fathers wanted and adhere very closely to our Constitution. Take notes, research the voting records of politicians, analyze, and vote intelligently in the future elections, regardless of your political party.

SOCIAL SECURITY

The last factor that affects your American Dream is the one that breaks my heart the most, because many elderly have placed hope and dependency in Social Security. When President Roosevelt's administration developed and created the Social Security Administration, it was not meant to be a retirement shelter. It was developed to assist the American people, not a retirement fund, during the time of the depression and was not meant to go bankrupt. My intention is to make a short mention of this "Social Security retirement benefit" because a great number of senior Americans count on this benefit when they reach an advanced age. Additionally, President Lyndon B. Johnson signed into law Medicare, which goes hand in hand with Social Security in order to assist our senior population defray the cost of medical care.

The way Social Security was developed to receive the funds to compliment a retirement plan is through continuous contributions from all workers in the nation. It is a vicious cycle, that although not a perfect system in principal, funds went out for "retirees," from active workers. The "geniuses" in Washington, as with everything else they touch, have been able to subtract the life expectancy of these funds by borrowing money for other social programs and pet projects, without repaying what they borrowed. Compounded by the extended life expectancy of the American people, benefits will be required to be paid for a longer period. What politicians have committed is a crime, by either stopping this benefit or reducing the amount of entitlement for those that receive the benefit. Furthermore, it is a double crime to inform those that have paid into the system for decades; they are not entitled to any benefits because the system is out of funds. Politicians in Washington continue to commit atrocities against our senior citizens, after they have paid into the system most of their lives. It is a continuous abuse, because they are not made aware of their dubious practices against a fund, which has been paid for by the American worker, as well as cutting benefits. At least they should have the decency to make the younger generation aware of the bankruptcy of the system, to allow them the option of finding another way to secure a retirement. It seems that in order to continue payment of those that have earned the benefit or paid for their retirement, they continue the abuse by collecting payments into a bankrupt system.

For decades, politicians from both parties have "borrowed" money from the Social Security funds to finance other social and political pet programs, without the approval from those who paid into the system. These funds have been used like the personal "piggy bank" of politicians from both parties but the funds have never been returned or allocated back to the Social Security from the federal budget. This practice has contributed to the reduction of the "life expectancy" of the Social Security Administration, because they have withdrawn more funds than what those who contribute have been able to replace. The prediction is that Social Security will run out of funds within the next thirty years or less, roughly by the year 2037. At present, with the economy the way it is and the unemployment situation, this prediction might be shorter. There are less employee contributions to the funds and more individuals receiving benefits, with even more scheduled to receive benefits in the next five to ten years. The only way these funds will be extended, is if we use a socialist approach or the Robin Hood principle that you take away from the rich to provide to the poor. In other words, those who need more receive more benefits based on their income, than those whose income is higher and are in less need of Social Security benefits. Regardless of what you input into the system, the government will make the decision of how much you are entitled to, based on necessity or income. Americans will go out of their way to help their fellow Americans, but it should not be as everything is nowadays with the government, where things are shoved down your throat. It is also sad that the head of the Social Security Administration, which is a political appointee, and the management of the agency leave much to be desired because of mismanagement of the agency. A good example of this mismanagement is the outrageous expenditures for management training seminars in luxurious resorts, as reported by the news media. It seems that the prediction of bankruptcy means nothing to politicians in Washington or the heads of the Social Security Administration, because all we have to do is print more money and Washington will fix everything like magic. Like everything else in Washington, it is business as usual to spend your hard-earned money and not care about the outcome of the ordinary citizens of the nation.

A common excuse that politicians make is the fact that the "baby boomers" are getting ready to reach retirement age, will apply for Social Security benefits and will subtract the years left to pay benefits to contributors. The solution would be to allocate the borrowed funds back to the Administration, but like everything else in Washington you cannot track monies wasted and they really do not care about what happens to the little people. It seems that part of the solution suggested by the politicians is to increase or extend the retirement age for a few more years, which will be higher than sixty-seven, in order to reduce the number of qualifiers for this supplemental benefit. Maybe they are hoping that many seniors will pass away and that way they have fewer seniors to pay. This is conceivable, because nobody knows what politicians think or do and you cannot believe what they say. Another "great idea" by some politicians was to allow beneficiaries to invest a portion of their benefits into the stock market in order to minimize the amount payable by Social Security. The way the stock market is going lately, lack of knowledge, and the way certain corporations are going bankrupt, it is not a great idea. This has been their only great idea in Washington, when this idea did pass through Congress. Politicians have created a "five-headed monster" by using the funds for other pet project and social programs in the first place. They do not have a solid solution to the present problem that they have created. If you are under the age of fifty-five, my advice to you is to, start finding a way to participate in an employer retirement plan or, save your last penny and do not count on any type of benefit from Social Security. This supplemental benefit to your retirement will be nonexistent when you get to age sixty-five or whatever age the politicians set as a retirement age. If it is available, you will have to work until age ninety, if you do not pass away prior to reaching that magic golden age of retirement. It is hard to comprehend that we take care of some "able bodies" in our population who do not want to work and reject the notion of taking care of those who have worked all their lives when they reach that golden age. Additionally, it is amazing that we take care of financial institutions and the auto industry, but neglect to take care of a sector of the population that has paid and earned a benefit, which is Social Security. Politicians have taken the senior population for granted in all elections and expect seniors to continue to re-elect them into office. Politicians should be made aware that the senior population keeps themselves abreast of what goes on in Washington and are intelligent enough, not senile, to make a difference in the elections. Percentage wise, they are the largest, constant voting population in the nation because it consists of about sixteen percent that religiously goes to the polls. A good idea would be to take notes and organize in order to vote out of office those politicians that conduct business as usual in Washington. If workers unions organize to support politicians and elect all them into office when they take care of them, seniors can do the same to vote them out of office. All seniors should organize as their only option to vote out all those politicians that are not fighting for their best interest in Washington. The senior population is the largest block of voters in the nation and should stop voting with their hearts and elect those true representatives and not re-elect all that dead wood in Washington. What seniors should do is organize and demand the same amount of "bailouts" for Social Security as those approved by Congress for special interests, in order to extend the life expectancy of Social Security, until a solution to the problem is found and passed into law. Seniors should demand from politicians in Washington their rights and the benefits that they have earned and worked so hard for all their lives.

The added benefit of Medicare, to assist to defray medical expenses, has placed the funds in jeopardy because of the high cost of medical care, mismanagement of the benefit, fraud and abuse and extensive medical care and attention for our senior population, which requires immediate attention. Although the cost of medical care has rocketed uncontrollably in the last decade, fraud and abuse by unscrupulous personnel in the medical profession, frivolous lawsuits by trial lawyers and abuse of insurance companies have been the number one contributor to the dangers of bankruptcy of this benefit. This abuse has been discovered for decades, but it continues to date because of lack of intervention by politicians in Congress. For years, the practice of double or triple billing and outrageous charges for routine medical visits have resulted in a detriment to the Administration, but no oversight from our representatives has been even worse. Our representatives in Congress have not taken corrective action or done anything due to their personal agenda to protect trial lawyers because of political support, special interest groups, and the agenda to socialize the medical care in the nation. Although I do not have any interest in a particular political party because to me all politicians are alike, the left has always wanted to socialize the medical care in the nation for decades. This has been in the mill for the past three decades, but we are not so dumb that we cannot figure this out and our seniors are too frustrated and afraid to do anything about it. It is my opinion that they have attempted to eliminate the medical portion of Social Security with this hidden agenda of social medicine, and they are at the verge of having their wish come true. Politicians claim that the Medicare system is billions of dollars in debt, but members of both parties have done nothing to correct the problems. They have always turned a blind eye, because it does not fit into their hidden agenda. Now that the system is in shambles, they have the excuse to eliminate Medicare, reduce or eliminate benefits and incorporate every participating senior into a government-controlled medical system. Let us hope and pray that they do not create a larger one, instead of fixing the problem, as is standard procedure for politicians in Washington. Once we have social medicine, the cost will escalate because everybody will take this option, the government bureaucracy, shortage of physicians and the cost will be exuberant because the average citizen will opt for the free medical care. In their way to justify the approval of this legislation or bill, they come with magical numbers of the population without medical care. This includes even illegal immigrants, when they receive medical care in hospital emergency rooms, although they deny this as being part of the legislation. As I have discussed in a previous chapter, the American's "golden heart" is starting to tarnish because there should be an end to carry on our back everyone that comes to this nation illegally and taxpayers to defray the cost of their needs. It will be cheaper to send funds to their country of origin and enforce the current immigration laws, rather than treating them here, and provide for their daily needs with social programs. It is true that the health care system in this nation is in need of a complete overhaul, but we should start by amending the process slowly, part by part. We should not try to pass another lightning legislation and create a monster that we will not be able to handle in the future and have a larger portion of the population without medical care. We should start by enrolling those who qualify for Medicaid, and those that do not want medical insurance to leave them alone. This is a nation of choices and freedom and the government should not force citizens to do something that they do not want to do. We do not need politicians in Washington to dictate or think for all the citizens in the nation. Those that refuse medical insurance should be required to pay as they go for any medical need that they require, and quit being everybody's keeper. Again, this is a nation of choices and the wrong choice should come with consequences. We have reached the point in our lives that we should stop the dependency on the federal government. Services should be refused or denied to those that fail to comply with any type of medical care.

It is fair to make a clarification that people have the misconception that Supplemental Social Income (SSI) and Medicaid are not payable from the funds from the Social Security Administration. This benefit is for the disabled, or to supplement an individual's income, who are not able to work on a full time basis. The same applies to the Medical Care Program (Medicaid) which is a social program to defray the cost of medical care for individuals and families of individuals, that lack medical insurance or unable to pay for medical insurance because of their income. Although in some cases individuals are required to co-pay for this medical assistance if based on income, the cost is minimal because it is based on income. These benefits are payable from funds allocated by the federal government, from taxes paid by employees, employers and the state where the individual or family resides. I make this clarification because although the Social Security Administration monitors part of the programs, they have nothing to do with or affect your retirement benefits from the Social Security.

If you wonder how this affects your American Dream, the majority of Americans see the Social Security as their sole form of retirement. The reason this happens is lack of knowledge, type of employment, educational level, or type of income they receive from their employment. This will prevent them from making other arrangements or saving for their retirement and creates headaches at the most vulnerable years of their lives. You must remember the intention for the Social Security retirement; it was created as a supplement to your "real" retirement. You cannot count on these monies as a sole form of retirement. Plan a good retirement through your place of employment, if they have a 401-K, start saving. Buy a good life insurance that you can cash in at maturity or if you want to take a chance, invest in the stock market, Certificates of Deposit (CD), any type of bond that yields some interest at maturity or just put your money in a savings account, if you have the control not to touch it. What is sad is the people that depend the most on this benefit, live from paycheck to paycheck and their saving habit or power is nonexistent. With the amount of Social Security retirement benefits you receive, it is not enough to defray your living expenses; you must work a part-time job to earn enough money to cover all these expenses. You cannot stop working when you retire under the Social Security retirement plan. I am not a financial advisor, but you should find a good and honest advisor to guide you to plan your retirement. You must understand that if you are under the age of fifty-five, (I use this age because politicians will increase the retirement age at their will), and to qualify for Social Security they will "grandfather" individuals of certain age before they change the requirements. At the rate we are going, the Social Security Administration might not exist when you reach age sixty, at least that is what is forecasted. For certain, your children and grandchildren will only know about Social Security, as a grandfather story or if it is included in the educational history curriculum. Our friends in Washington, the ones we vote into office to represent us, have done it to us one more time. I cannot count my blessings, because it is a vicious cycle, and they will do it to us repeatedly.

The same rule applies to the Medicare program because it is currently billions of dollars in default. Fraud and abuse, in addition to the frivolous lawsuits by unscrupulous trial lawyers to take advantage of a broken system, have been the reason why this program is close to extinction. Our elected officials in Washington, from both parties, have not taken corrective action to find a solution to the problem. It has been known that the hidden agenda from administrations in the past was to create or establish social medicine in the nation. They use the excuse now, of the high cost of medical care and the extended life expectancy of our senior population. The politicians have made sure that they have taken care of special interest, by providing federal assistance in the form of government "bailouts," but have ignored the Social Security Administration and Medicare, benefits that our seniors have religiously contributed. The problem has compounded, now the new generations of "baby boomers" are ready to start applying for these benefits, because the life expectancy of all seniors has risen. It is my opinion that politicians, by borrowing money from these funds, never paid them back because they did not think the life expectancy of seniors would pass age seventy or seventy-five. They have created a ten-headed monster and now do not know how to tackle it. Although, they have found a valid excuse to execute their hidden agenda, of creating a national social medicine program. This will complicate the whole medical system of the nation because of the myriad of complications, ranging from shortage of physicians, lack of competition from medical plans, to the lack of investment for medical research by private industry. In Additional, complications include higher taxes and penalties to individuals and private industry, government bureaucracy, and an increase in the deficit because of the cost of full participation in the government program, would create a free ride for everyone. It is worth highlighting that the frivolous suits by trial lawyers, one of the reasons for high medical care cost, will continue against the federal government because with this new medical system some physicians will be federal employees. As you all know, this special interest group is protected by politicians, due to their political support and because birds of a feather flock together.

My advice to seniors is to organize and demand from politicians what is rightfully theirs, as they have earned and worked hard most their lives for these benefits. As one of the biggest voting block in every election cycle, they should refuse to re-elect those politicians that do not have their best interest at heart when they get to Washington. The real change is with your vote because this is the best weapon you have against corruption of politicians, activist organizations, and special interest in Washington. You are extremely intelligent and have to start voting with your brain and stop politicians of both parties from taking you for granted. You deserve better. Refuse to be taken as if you were senile and unable to think for yourself. You do not need to be controlled by or have politicians thinking for you, because contrary to what they think, you are not dumb and are able to make decisions in your best interest. There is plenty of time to recover our nation from corrupted politicians who only have their greed, thirst for power and own interest in mind. If they are not able to represent you and refuse to hear your voice as a block of constituents, get rid of them. Legislation is only around the corner where you are going to lose more and more benefits that you have work so hard and paid your monies. Just open your eyes and ears, stay vigilant and voice your opinion loud and clear, because it does count. Do not allow politicians and special interests to classify you as expendables, because you still have a lot to live for.

EPILOGUE

I hope that I have accomplished my goal to bring to the attention of the American people that we must take charge of our lives, prepare ourselves educationally, look forward to be successful, achieve our American Dream, and be part of the solution to route this country in the right direction. There is plenty of time to make the necessary changes and make things better. In simple terminology, I have tried to bring to the attention of the American people the eight most important issues that affect our lives in this great nation. It has not been my intention to insult or diminish the level of intelligence of any group of Americans, but to remind them that we have to assume the role of responsibility in our lives.

We should return to our basic principles, take control of our children by instilling the proper behavior and morality, and be the pillars of our families and our communities. We should prepare our children for a brighter future and to be responsible citizens. We have allowed our children to dictate and set the rules in our family units, due to either apathy or the need to work outside of the home due to financial obligations. It is time to give our children tough love because they will appreciate it in the future when they are able to see what we wanted for them – a better future. We have empowered babysitters and daycare centers to assume our duties as parents. Additionally, we have taken lightly what is expected of us as parents and the lifetime commitment of bringing a child into this world.

Although our educational system is in shambles, it is mostly because of lack of parental participation and the responsibility to demand from our children educational excellence. We use our schools as a daycare center and the teachers as babysitters during the time we are at our jobs. We should demand that our children's teachers have the best qualifications, maintaining these skills up to date. We fail to follow-up on our children's schoolwork and progress and do not ensure that our children have the basic concepts of reading, writing, analyzing, and mathematics. These subjects are of utmost importance and needed in any decision or direction we want to take our lives. This affects our educational system from elementary, high school and institutions of higher learning. They have been instrumental in the formation and in all the decisions that all American people take as adults in their lives. Lack of basic education not only affects our lives, but the lives of other citizens in the nation as a whole. This will give us independence, pride and a sense of value.

Immigrants of all backgrounds, race, and creed built this country. Americans have a "heart of gold" and are always willing to open their arms to everyone who arrives in this land. The American people have always welcomed legal immigration because it has never been a burden to the nation and our citizens. The problem is that illegal immigration has grown out of control, to the point that it is swallowing us like quicksand. Our representatives in Washington have ignored the problem for decades and the only solution they have offered is "amnesty." What they use to sugarcoat the problem is "comprehensive immigration laws" every few years. They refuse to secure our borders and every thirty years we have to pass the same laws to appease the largest growing population in the nation, to win their votes. They have become a detriment to our federal budget due to social programs, all types of crimes are on the rise, and politicians do not offer a real solution to these problems. This problem is affecting our lives at all levels and parts of the nation. We, as a nation, need to stop thinking with our hearts and start thinking with our brains as to how this will affect us. This nation can no longer assimilate millions of illegal immigrants into our lives without it affecting the lives and future of our children. We must do something about the immigration laws and enforce them vigorously.

One of the factors affecting your American Dream is the United States economy. This has been the greatest teaching experience for most Americans, because we were complacent and never thought our politicians or the financial system would fail us. Regardless of whose fault it is, we must be prepared for a long recovery period. We must follow the advice of some "wise financial advisors" that we should have enough money saved to cover at least six months of our required debt payments. The greed of financial institutions, and executive officers, compounded with the lack of oversight from our Legislative System, has been the major contributors to the collapse of the economy. It is time to stop pointing fingers of guilt and find a solution to the problem. Our elected officials, from both parties, are guilty as charged because they orchestrated the collapse of the housing market. Although they continue to use the excuse that they inherited problems from the previous administration, some of them have been in Congress for the past thirty years. Let us hope they do not do it to us again. Once you take charge of any institution or organization, you are responsible for the good, the bad, or the ugly and do not find excuses or blame anybody else. If you want the job you can have it, but fix whatever is wrong and take credit for whatever goes right. The people on Wall Street, in conjunction with all financial institutions, must be legislated and watched constantly because greed is the worst thing that a person can have. Another lesson that you should learn is that if you do not know how to play the game, do not play. If you do not have money to spare, do not invest or gamble with the stock market, because you might lose your savings or retirement in the end. You are the best person to be in charge of your money. If you were not born into money, stop thinking that you will become a millionaire by "playing the market." Save and diversify your money in different banks because they are insured, but please do not put it under the mattress. As Americans, we should pull together and fight to get this economy going regardless of the mistakes we have made to send some fools to Washington to be our representatives. Learn from your mistakes but please do not make the same mistake twice. Please think before you act and you will be safe in your future plans. The golden rules are to pay as you go; do not buy what you cannot afford and read before you sign on the dotted line or what you commit yourself.

The population in the United States of America has lost the habit of reading newspapers due to the era of electronics and technology. It has started from our early training years where reading is non-existent and television is not only entertainment, but also a means to take care of our children. We have the tendency to receive all the news from the television or internet. Consequently, major newspapers as well as the small towns, are on the verge of going bankrupt. The electronic era, compounded with political bias from certain "journalists," have targeted and divided a part of the population based on political ideology. Ergo, the sales of newspapers have declined. Catchy phrases from "newscasters" have turned from opinions to truths and influenced the great majority of Americans. This influence is reflected on how they elect government officials, regardless of political party. It is easier to listen than to read, analyze, and digest information to form a personal opinion. Although the American people are full of frustration, they have the tendency to be naïve in the way they elect their government officials. It seems that there is an inability to analyze issues and "weed out" reality from fiction. The tendency to vote with the heart, instead of the brain and common sense, has become the norm. Good speeches and promises do not equal results in our best interest after the campaigns are over. Additionally, they continue to elect and reelect, regardless of political party, the same individuals that have their own agenda instead of the best interest of the people who elect them. It is time that we demand time limits for the members of Congress, although they will not do it or listen to the people. It is not in their best interest to hold office for a maximum of three terms and out. This is the only way we are going to get the coveted change in legislation and government that we are looking for. We should organize and utilize the best weapon we have, which is our vote. It is time to stop overspending our tax money on pork projects from politicians of both parties. It is important to highlight that contrary to the opinion of many, the American people are intelligent and level-headed but frustrated and looking for real change which is something they yet to find. You have the real change at the reach of your arm and that is when you vote.

The United States Government was founded with good principles, by our founding fathers, and is the best system in the entire world. This is the true land of freedom and opportunities for everyone that comes to our nation. We do have flaws, but the only ones that can correct them are "we the people." This is supposed to be a system of checks and balances. We have not put this principle into effect in the past two decades. Out of frustration or lack of trust in the system, we have allowed the Executive, Legislative and Judicial systems to go haywire. We continue to elect and re-elect politicians that do not represent our interest in Washington. They do not legislate in the interest of the people, but in the interest of their political party. You have given them the power to think for us and convinced them the American people are not smart enough to analyze what they are doing in Washington. Politicians think that they are above the law and us and their only interest is to be re-elected. They spend our tax money like if it was play money and have gotten us into the biggest debt in the history of this nation. They continue to fund activist organizations and social programs that do not support the interest of the majority of the people. Some of the governmental social programs promote dependency on the federal government and laziness. We have lost respect around the world where third world nations thumb their noses at us. The power of our currency is not what it used to be because of our debt around the world. The excuse the politicians use is the "blame game" in which always the previous party in power was the guilty one and they left the country in shambles. We are supposed to elect people that will take charge, solve our problems, and not give us excuses. All politicians are made from the same mold and you take a chance when you cast your vote and elect one. We should demand term limits for elected officials, the Supreme Court, and all political appointees should be confirmed in order for them not to become dead wood or too powerful for their own good. Please do not prostitute your vote for some pork money. Do not believe that you do not have the capacity to make a sound decision, because the American people are intelligent and capable to take control of their lives. Be independent from the federal government and do not allow politicians to control your life by being a leech of federal social programs. When you vote, do it with your brain and not your heart; organize in order to make a difference and obtain the real change that is best for you and your family. Do not allow false promises from politicians to come true because they do not care about your future or that of the nation. If you want to register as a voter of a specific political party, that is your choice but vote on the issues not on party lines. Do not be violent but fight with the best weapon you have, which is your vote.

Last, but not least, is the statutes of the Social Security Administration in which the top management has started to spend our funds as if it was their own. We should realize that this is not a retirement shelter but a supplement to our retirement plan. It was not meant to be a retirement plan, especially when politicians transferring funds from Social Security Administration to defray costs of other social programs have driven the entity into bankruptcy. We should plan ahead for our future through our best years in the working force participating in a 401K plan. At the rate the Social Security Administration is heading, all those under age fifty-five will see no benefits from this agency regardless of how much money they contribute into it. It is forecasted to go bankrupt by the year 2037 unless a miracle happens or they start implementing the "Robin Hood" principle and give to those that contributed less, but need more. Not fair, but this is our government and politicians make the rules. We have to wise up and plan ahead to have a good future in our most vulnerable years.

Medicare and Health Care is another monster of five heads that politicians want to control. The want to socialize our medical system and they are not able to solve the "biggest monster" they have with Medicare. They should slow down and correct the present problems before they get involved in something they cannot handle. If the majority of Americans are happy with the medical insurance plan they have, just find the solution to the ones that do not have a plan or do not want one.

We should stop and analyze the situation the nation is presently in and the future we are facing. The politicians of both parties are taking us into the land of no return with all the debt that they are creating for our children, grandchildren, and us. We should not allow the government to take control of our lives and make us dependent on the system. We should put a stop to over taxation, so politicians can achieve their pet projects. Again, stop re-electing corrupt politicians that do not represent us in Washington and whose only loyalty is to their political party and special interests. You must remember that politicians are the same, no matter to what party they belong. Please read and analyze before you cast your vote to elect or re-elect men and women who do not care what happens to you or your family. We are no longer the great super power we use to be and at the rate we are going, we will soon be a colony of China. Enough is enough and we have the obligation to put a stop to this abuse, because we deserve and should demand the best.

www.ingramcontent.com/pod-product-compliance
Lightning Source LLC
Chambersburg PA
CBHW051438280526
45785CB00003B/1342